To my dear "Norar
Jack ... May
with the perfect peace of Christ!
You have blessed me in many ways
dear friend!

Eternal Mysteries Of Christ
Revealed In God's Plan For You.

*...and I will give to each one a white stone, and on the stone
will be engraved a new name that no one knows except
the one who receives it. Revelation 2:17 NLT.*

• . . Now may God bless you know & always, Terry
Your friend . . . Hank

Rev. Hank Van Zyderveld

March, 2012

xulon
PRESS

Bible Versions

The majority of Scriptures quoted within this book are taken from the New King James Version of the Bible, Copyright © 1982, Thomas Nelson, Inc. All rights reserved. All other Scriptures quoted, are from one or more of the following Bible translations, and will be indicated as such when appropriate.

Concordant Literal New Testament, third printing. Copyright © 1983 by Concordant Publishing Concern. All rights reserved.

J.P. Green's Literal Translation Scripture taken from the Literal Translation of the Holy Bible (LITV); Copyright © 1976 - 2000; By Jay P. Green, Sr.; Used by permission of the copyright holder; Courtesy of Sovereign Grace Publishers and Christian Literature World.

The King James Version. (Authorized)

The Message: The Bible in Contemporary Language This edition issued by contractual arrangement with NavPress, a

Articles written by other authors included in this book will be noted as being quoted, printed in bold italics and identified with their name in the end notes whenever possible.

To underscore the fact that Heaven and Hell are proper nouns, and Satan a real spiritual entity, I have intentionally chosen to capitalize them throughout this book, as I would other proper nouns. When referring to The Holy Spirit of God or God's Holy Spirit, I will refer to Him in a more personal way as Holy Spirit, denoting that Holy Spirit is a special and unique part of God–operating distinctly within the Godhead. When referring to God, Jesus, or Holy Spirit as He, Him, His or Himself, I have chosen to use capitalization.

www.xulonpress.com

Dedication

This book is dedicated to the God of Abraham, Isaac and Jacob, Jesus Christ, and Holy Spirit. All honor, glory, and praise belongs to each of you!

May the quest for truth be our clarion call. Now is the time to rise up and seize hold of our Kingdom inheritance, and the promises that God our Father through His Son, Jesus Christ has for all who are seeking truth. It is our destiny to claim the promises that He has for us.

May you find truth and freedom within these pages, and may they have a profound everlasting effect upon you. This invitation is extended to every person regardless of nationality, ethnic origin, or religious affiliation. All are welcome.

This is a faithful saying and worthy of all acceptance. For to this end we both labor and suffer reproach, because we trust in the living God, who is the Savior of all men, especially of those who believe. These things command and teach. 1 Timothy 4:9–11.

About The Author

Hank Van Zyderveld was born into a fine Dutch Heritage. He was raised in the Christian Reformed tradition, but not limited to that expression. Hank is amazed at how God moves in the lives of individuals regardless of their denominational/non-denominational affiliations. He believes that testing and tasting the goodness of God through all of the various expressions of Christian faith produces opportunity for tremendous spiritual growth. Hank loves seeking the Lord through the prophetic in its purist form, having no fear in asking his heavenly Father for the hidden deeper truths of Christ.

For the past thirty three years and counting, Hank continues to work in a secular environment as a flexographic print press operator and die man. He loves the people and his work environment. He also has a love for motorcycles. On a warm sunny day, he can be found out on the highways and byways with his dear wife Monika, cruising into one adventure after another.

Hank loves encouraging people to consider the importance of how God sees them from His eternal perspective. It was from out of that zeal that he has recently pursued the opportunity to become an ordained minister of the gospel of Jesus Christ. He now holds his credentials through Abba Ministries of Canada. Hank is trusting the Lord to continue ordering his steps, wherever they may lead.

Acknowledgments

Monika is the love of my life. She is my steadfast best friend and precious wife of thirty two years. Together, we have five beautiful children, and our first grandchild. Our children are Robert, Leanne and her husband Jason, Briella (their new born baby girl), Randall, David, and Sharlane. Each one a unique gift from God.

Monika and I are pleased to also acknowledge our parents, extended family members, friends, and co-workers. Each of you has helped shape our character by your personal influence knowingly or unknowingly. We are grateful for the part that each of you has played in our personal lives, and are looking forward to a continuation of your input, influence and support.

During my studies, while collecting my thoughts and preparing notes for the writing of this book, many confirmations came to me, indicating that I was on the right track. Those confirmations came from the very heart of God and the works of several anointed authors. One example of two such authors are David and Zoe Sulem. They will be introduced to you, along with the others as we go along.

An interesting point to keep in mind–is that there really is nothing new under the sun. Whatever revelation we may receive concerning truth, can actually be traced back to before the foundation of time.

Journey For Truth

It is my prayer that as a man, I stay true to my convictions in the writing of this book, but more than anything else, I desire to be a servant and friend of the King.

Sir Winston Churchill is reported to have said, **I quote;** *"Sometimes in the course of history some men occasionally stumble onto truth. Most, however are able to pick themselves up, dust themselves off, and be on their way again just as if nothing has happened."* **End of quotation.**

A wise man once said, **I quote;** *"The hardest thing you will ever do, is to admit that you are wrong."* **End of quotation.**

I personally have been wrong on many occasions concerning truth, and still may often be wrong. The challenge then, is to continue searching for truth until it is found.May there be found within these pages, truth that enables us to achieve new levels of faith, maturity and peace.

For example, when we allow God's perfect peace to fill our soul, it will expel any fear or anxiety that may be operating within our lives–especially fear and anxiety we may have concerning our final resting state, and that of our loved ones.

Rev. Hank Van Zyderveld
Abbotsford, British Columbia, Canada.
2012

Introduction

Dear Friends, I believe that it will be to your benefit to read the topics contained within this book in the order in which they are being presented. It is my desire for you to be led specifically this way, by the intentional arrangement of each topic in the order that you find them. Rather than attempt to write a book that has a seamless contextual flow chapter by chapter, I have decided to let each chapter stand on its own merit. Hopefully the big picture of God's unfailing love for you, will begin to emerge and come forth through the examples of my personal testimony in such a way that together, we will be able to spring board from that point onward, diving deeper into the insights that I wish to share with you.

This book has been divided into two sections. Section "A" will be a brief introduction–detailing portions of my personal life experiences, and section "B" will deal with several core beliefs that I have come to embrace, based on inspiration and revelation that has come forth from out of those experiences.

I sincerely make no apology to anyone finding offence in any of the challenges as they are presented, or to anyone feeling that this book may be heretical. According to Easton's Bible Dictionary, heresy denotes division or schisms within the Church. A heretical person is one who follows his own self-willed agenda. Heresies thus signify self-chosen doctrines not emanating from God. 1 Corinthians 11:19; Titus 3:10; 2 Peter 2:1.

It is my prayer that the truth of God's Holy Word will

emanate through the work of Holy Spirit in such a way that we will undeniably be rescued from the religious traditions that have kept so many in bondage and self condemnation.

God desires for each of us to experience total freedom from religious bondage through the ministry of reconciliation and restoration. This is the breakthrough the world and many in the Church are still waiting to experience for the first time! Our heavenly Father has prepared a future time soon approaching, when all of His family is finally and fully restored back into an everlasting loving relationship with Him through His Son Jesus Christ.

Sadly and tragically for the past sixteen hundred plus years, those in Christendom have been indoctrinated into the things of God without the option to even bring into question the validity of perceived interpretations of Scripture as taught by the "powers that be" from within the early Church. Persuasive instruction typically began at an early age without much chance for the traditional status-quo to ever change.

Within early Church history, deliberate corruption of the translated Word of God was already beginning to take place. Pagan religious leaders from that era began to wield powerful control over the masses. For example, specific promises from God concerning the Jewish People were forcefully taken from them, and then spiritualized for the Churches benefit instead. This is called replacement theology. We are still suffering the effects of this spiritual apostasy to this day. The Church will not be able to flow in the full anointing of God's favor, until she begins to recognize this fact. The body of Christ (the Church) is called by God to be a blessing to His ancient covenant people–the Jews. We are commanded in Scripture to; *"Pray for the peace of Jerusalem"* ...so that we may prosper. This is not meant just corporately, but individually as well. We are also instructed in the Holy Bible to; *"Test all things."* Could the *"Working out of our salvation with fear and trembling,"* be a significant part of our responsibility in the ongoing quest for truth, by the very testing of those things?

Because of doctrinal pride, stubbornness, or from a purely

practical business sense, there is a tremendous possibility that we may become unable or unwilling to re-think our theological positions as to what we believe. I can well imagine how difficult it might be for a minister of the gospel of Jesus Christ to renounce certain doctrine that he or she may have embraced or taught from the pulpit or from within the walls of well established religious learning institutions over decades of time!

It is not my intention to make an exhaustive theological study out of what I have just shared, or on each of the topics that will be covered in this book, due to its limited scope. I anticipate a broad readership that will range from those who are very learned in God's Holy Word, to those who are just starting out, and will include those who have no understanding at all concerning the things of God. John 21:25 speaks about exhaustive study this way; *And there are also many other things that Jesus did, which if they were written one by one, I suppose that even the world itself could not contain the books that would be written. Amen.*

For the benefit of those who may not have a Bible, I have included as many Bible passages as possible wherever needed, rather than just giving references to particular verses of Holy Scripture. This method however, is not meant to be exhaustive. I realize there may be difficulties in bringing balance to some aspects of truth as being presented in this book because of language and cultural differences. Truth must be presented in such a way that it becomes relevant to that specific culture without compromising said truth. For example, truth that was being taught to the Jewish people in biblical times was presented to them through the use of parables, allegories, and metaphors from a Hebraic perspective. Indigenous people need to be reached in like manner. With that being said, I am sensing that it will be a challenge to keep the ideas flowing smoothly as we go at times. I am however, committed to giving to you my best for God's glory and honor, as I place my trust in the leading of Holy Spirit.

There are those in prophetic ministry who have been

laboring and pressing in with prayer for the revealing of the next big event or new thing that has been spoken of often in recent times. The next big event or new thing is in fact the revealing of Father God's heart for humanity. This has always been the big event or new thing, and the very essence of true evangelism as based on 2 Corinthians 5:17–21; *... Therefore, if anyone is in Christ, he is a new creation; old things have passed away; behold, all things have become new. Now all things are of God, who has reconciled us to Himself through Jesus Christ, and has given us the ministry of reconciliation, that is, that God was in Christ reconciling the world to Himself, not imputing their trespasses to them, and has committed to us the word of reconciliation. Now then, we are ambassadors for Christ, as though God were pleading through us: we implore you on Christ's behalf, be reconciled to God. For He made Him who knew no sin to be sin for us, that we might become the righteousness of God in Him.*

I have found myself to be in a flux with some of the beliefs that I have personally held over time, including some things I currently believe while writing this book! As we are continually being challenged by God and by those around us, as to what we believe, we must not be afraid to re-evaluate some of those beliefs. We must persevere and press on to the high calling for truth. With this in mind, I welcome each and every one of you.

Let us journey together and discover the depths of God's amazing love that He has for each of us, starting with a look at the person of Jesus Christ. Hopefully you will discover as I have, who He claims to be. It is paramount for us to have a crystal clear understanding of His claims according to Scripture and discern whether those claims are true or not, otherwise the claims He makes concerning Himself become nothing more than worthless rhetoric.

For precept must be upon precept..., line upon line ..., here a little, there a little. Isaiah 28:10; *...He said to them, "Those who are well have no need of a physician, but those who are sick. I did not come to call the righteous, but sinners,* to repentance." Mark 2:17; *"Come now, and let us reason together,"* says the Lord, *"though your sins are like scarlet, they shall be as white as snow; though they are red like crimson, they shall be as wool."* Isaiah 1:18; *"I have other sheep, too, that are not in this sheepfold. I must bring them also, and they will listen to My voice; and there will be one flock with one Shepherd."* **John 10:16 NLT;** *For Christ Himself has made peace between us Jews and you Gentiles by making us all one people. He has broken down the wall of hostility that used to separate us. By His death He ended the whole system of Jewish law that excluded the Gentiles. His purpose was to make peace between Jews and Gentiles by creating in Himself one new person from the two groups. Together as one body, Christ reconciled both groups to God by means of His death, and our hostility toward each other was put to death. He has brought this Good News of peace to you Gentiles who were far away from Him, and to us Jews who were near.* Ephesians 2:14-17 NLT.

Contents

Section "A"

1

Finding No Fault In Jesus Christ

Jesus the Christ was and still is the most controversial historical person to ever walk on the face of the earth. It has been said of Him, that He was either the greatest liar that ever lived, or a raving lunatic, or as He claimed Himself, the Messiah, Son of the living God! To this very day, He continues to challenge the outer limits of our reasoning and understanding on a daily basis as He invites each of us to step out of our traditional theological security. He desires to take us away from a superficial comfort that cannot last, to a truly genuine comfort that can only be discovered when we come to rest completely in Him. This is one of the most amazing paradoxes of the ages. Jesus calls each of us out of our comfort and into the storms of life, so that we can begin to seek Him and contend for His perfect peace. He is the narrow gate that we all must enter in by. With the help of Holy Spirit, and with the promises found in God's Holy Word, I believe that ultimately none shall fail to enter in.

Pontius Pilate understood that Jesus Christ was not a liar, or a raving lunatic, but was claiming deity when He referred to Himself as the Son of God. The eternality of Jesus Christ is woven throughout all the Holy Scriptures. In John 1:1-4; 14 it says; *In the beginning was the Word, and the Word was with God, and the Word was God. He was in the beginning with God. All things were made through Him, and without Him nothing was made. In Him was life, and the life was the light of men... And the Word became flesh and dwelt among us, and we beheld his glory, the glory as of the only begotten of the Father, full of grace and truth.*

In the Old Testament Scriptures, we find the most amazing and accurate prophesies foretelling the advent of the Messiah hundreds of years in advance of His coming.

Isaiah 7:14. *Therefore the Lord Himself will give you a sign: behold, the virgin shall conceive and bear a Son, and shall call His name Immanuel.*

Micah 5:2. *But you, Bethlehem Ephrathah, though you are little among the thousands of Judah, yet out of you shall come forth to Me the one to be ruler in Israel, whose goings forth are from of old, from everlasting.*

Isaiah 53:3-9. *He is despised and rejected by men, a man of sorrows and acquainted with grief. And we hid, as it were, our faces from Him; He was despised, and we did not esteem Him. Surely He has borne our griefs and carried our sorrows; yet we esteemed Him stricken, smitten by God, and afflicted. But He was wounded for our transgressions, He was bruised for our iniquities; the chastisement for our peace was upon Him, and by His stripes we are healed. All we like sheep have gone astray; we have turned, every one, to his own way; and the Lord has laid on Him the iniquity of us all. He was oppressed and He was afflicted, yet He opened not His mouth; He was led as a lamb to the slaughter, and as a sheep before its shearers is silent, So He opened not His mouth. He was taken from prison and from judgment, and who will declare His generation? For He was cut off from the land of the living; for the transgressions of My people He was stricken. And they made His grave with the wicked, but with the rich at His death, because He had done no violence, nor was any deceit in his mouth.*

Luke 22: 66-70. *As soon as it was day, the elders of the*

people, both chief priests and scribes, came together and led Him into their council, saying, "If You are the Christ, tell us." But He said to them, "If I tell you, you will by no means believe. And if I also ask you, you will by no means answer me or let me go. Hereafter the Son of Man will sit on the right hand of the power of God." Then they all said, "Are You then the Son of God?" So He said to them, "You rightly say that I am." The Word of God teaches us some very important revelations concerning Jesus the Christ.

Jesus is all wise: *Now we are sure that You know all things, and have no need that anyone should question You. By this we believe that You came forth from God.* John 16:30.

Jesus is omnipresent: *..."and lo, I am with you always, even to the end of the age." Amen.* Matthew 28: 20.

Jesus is the supreme judge: *When Jesus saw their faith, He said to the paralytic, "Son, your sins are forgiven you."* Mark2:5.

Jesus is all powerful: *And Jesus came and spoke to them, saying, "All authority has been given to Me in Heaven and on earth."* Mathew 28:18.

Jesus Christ is the manifest Word of God. The Word is God, who came in the flesh of a man. This is made clear in the following passages.

The grass withers, the flower fades, But the word of our God stands forever. Isaiah 40: 8; *Heaven and earth will pass away, but My words will by no means pass away.* Mathew 24:35; *... The people answered Him, "We have heard from the law that the Christ remains forever..."* John 12:34; *Beware lest anyone cheat you through philosophy and empty deceit, according to the tradition of men, according to the basic principles of the world, and not according to Christ. For in Him dwells all the fullness of the Godhead bodily; and you are complete in Him, who is the head of all principality and power.* Colossians 2:8-10; *This is a faithful saying and worthy of all acceptance, that Christ Jesus came into the world to save sinners, of whom I am chief.* 1 Timothy 1:15; *For this is good and acceptable in the sight of God our Savior.* 1 Timothy

2:3; *And without controversy great is the mystery of godliness: God was manifested in the flesh, Justified in the Spirit, Seen by angels, Preached among the Gentiles, Believed on in the world, Received up in glory.* 1 Timothy 3:16; *For to this end we both labor and suffer reproach, because we trust in the living God, who is the Savior of all men, especially of those who believe.* 1Timothy 4:10; *...that they may adorn the doctrine of God our Savior in all things.* Titus 2:10; *... looking for the blessed hope and glorious appearing of our great God and Savior Jesus Christ.* Titus 2:13; *But when the kindness and the love of God our Savior toward man appeared.* Titus 3:4; *Then He said to Thomas, "Reach your finger here, and look at My hands; and reach your hand here, and put it into My side. Do not be unbelieving, but believing." And Thomas answered and said to Him, "My Lord and my God!" Jesus said to him, "Thomas, because you have seen Me, you have believed. Blessed are those who have not seen and yet have believed."* John 20: 27-29.

After considering these Scripture passages, over time I have come to believe and prayerfully you will as well, that Jesus the Christ is in fact, God the Almighty One, who came to us clothed in complete humility, leaving His heavenly domain so that He could dwell among humanity in the flesh as the perfect God man. He is the living Word, becoming the perfect atoning sacrifice for our sin and the sins of the entire world. God's incomprehensible plan of ultimate reconciliation and restoration was carefully preordained by His design. Holy Spirit and the pre-incarnate Christ were united in perfect harmony with God long before this world was ever created. *He indeed was foreordained before the foundation of the world, but was manifest in these last times for you.* 1 Peter 1:20.

God the Creator had no other plan. Satan is a created foe that in no possible way whatsoever could ever frustrate God's plans, thus forcing God to come up with a plan "B" option concerning the future of humanity.

2

A Deeper Truth

Some say that the deep mysteries of God are His and too lofty for our understanding, therefore un-necessary to pursue. I however, disagree. The deep mysteries of God are waiting to be revealed to those who desire to search them out. It is pleasing to God when we take an active interest in the pursuit of His deep mysteries. Through the art of discovery, I believe that we have the opportunity for something profoundly eternal to be forged deep within our spiritual D.N.A.

Randy Alcorn in his book titled: "Heaven,"[1] has something very interesting to say about revelatory insight in one of his opening remarks. Although his book is written specifically about Heaven, I believe that his opening remarks on revelatory insight can be applied to the insights that I desire to convey to each of you, my readers. He begins by sharing with his readers what a pastor visiting his office had to say to him one day. **I quote;**

"A pastor visiting my office asked what I was writing. "A big book on Heaven," I said. "Well," he replied, "since Scripture says, "No eye has seen, no ear has heard, no mind has conceived what God has prepared for those who love Him," what will you be talking about? Obviously, we can't know what God has prepared for us in Heaven." (He was referring to 1 Corinthians2:9 NIV).

I said to him what I always say: "You didn't complete the sentence. You also have to read verse ten." Here's how the complete sentence reads: "No eye has seen, no ear has heard, no mind has conceived what God has prepared for those who love Him – but God has revealed it to us by His Spirit." The context makes it clear that this revelation is God's Word (v.13), which tells us what God has prepared for us... Other verses are likewise pulled out to derail discussions about Heaven. For example, "The secret things belong to the Lord our God" Deuteronomy 29:29. *Heaven is regarded as a "secret thing." But the rest of the verse–again, rarely quoted–completes the thought: "But the things revealed belong to us and our children forever."*

We should accept that many things about Heaven are secret and that God has countless surprises in store for us. But as for the things God has revealed to us about Heaven, these things belong to us and our children. It's critically important that we study and understand them. That is precisely why God revealed them to us!

Another "silencer" is 2 Corinthians 12:2-4. *Paul says that fourteen years earlier he was "caught up to paradise," where he "heard inexpressible things, things that man is not permitted to tell." Some people use this verse to say we should not discuss what Heaven will be like. But all it says is that God didn't permit Paul to talk about his visit to Heaven. In contrast, God commanded the apostle John to talk about his prolonged visit to Heaven, which he did in detail in the book of Revelation. Likewise, Isaiah and Ezekiel wrote about what they saw in Heaven.*

Although it's inappropriate for us to speculate on what Paul might have seen in Heaven, it's certainly appropriate to discuss what John saw, because God chose to reveal it to us. If He didn't intend for us to understand it, why would He bother telling us about it? When was the last time you wrote someone a letter using word's you didn't expect them to comprehend? So, we should study, teach, and discuss God's revelation about Heaven given to us in His Word. Isaiah 55:9

*is another verse often cited in support of a "don't ask, don't tell" approach to Heaven: "As the heavens are higher than the earth, so are My ways higher than your ways and My thoughts higher than your thoughts." God's thoughts are indeed higher than ours, but when He reduces His thoughts into words and reveals them in Scripture, He expects us to study them, meditate on them, and understand them–again, not exhaustively, but accurately.*End of quotation.

With that being said, I humbly acknowledge that God may choose to conceal His deep mysteries from us, or He may choose to reveal them to us as He pleases through parables, allegories, metaphors, and similitudes.

Noah Webster's New International Dictionary of the English Language defines *Parable: 1. A short story that contains a moral or lesson. 2. A comparison; a similitude; specifically, a short fictitious narrative of something which might really occur in life or nature, by means of which a moral is drawn; as, the parables of Christ. Allegory: 1. A figurative discourse, in which the principal subject is described by another subject; a parable. The real subject is thus kept out of view, and we are left to collect the intentions of the writer or speaker by the resemblance of the secondary to the primary subject. 2. Anything which represents by suggestive resemblance; an emblem. 3. A figure representation which has a meaning beyond notion directly conveyed by the object painted or sculptured. Metaphor: 1. A figure of speech in which a word or phrase literally denoting one kind of object or idea is used in place of another to suggest a likeness or analogy between them (as in drowning in money); broadly: figurative language 2. An object, activity, or idea treated as a metaphor. At that time Jesus answered and said, "I thank You, Father, Lord of Heaven and earth, that You have hidden these things from the wise and prudent and have revealed them to babes. Even so, Father, for so it seemed good in Your sight. All things have been delivered to Me by My Father, and no one knows the Son except the Father. Nor does anyone know the Father except the Son, and the one to whom the Son wills to reveal*

Him. Matthew 11:25-27.

I realize that it can be very discomforting to venture out from the traditional status-quo of the familiar and ordinary, and yet venturing out can be very exhilarating, revelational, and rewarding. With this in mind, I invite you to come with me through an open door of opportunity. I believe that this open door will lead us into a gallery of new discoveries, and deeper insight. I suspect that some will reject any new thoughts or insight, while others remain indifferent. Regardless of where you may be at, please come along and journey with me. I trust that God will show His grace and mercy toward us, and that He will keep us from falling away.

When truth begins to penetrate the very essence of man's ego, it will affect his thoughts and any preconceived beliefs that he may have. Pride within man's ego has the capability of stopping the velocity of truth's impact. Pride is a very powerful aspect of our spirit that controls much of our emotions, feelings, and actions. Pride has always been the root cause of man's problems. Pride hinders our ability to receive forgiveness, and to forgive those who may have hurt us, or from admitting that we may be wrong concerning something. Pride will always exalt itself above truth. When our emotions have been damaged, or if we have been physically harmed, this can allow for a door to open within our heart. Once that door is opened, our hearts can become hardened, thus allowing pride to begin its destructive work. We must not allow room for pride to gain entry, because the negative effects of pride are so enormous. Proverbs 16:18, 19 says; *Pride goes before destruction, and a haughty spirit before a fall. Better to be of a humble spirit with the lowly, than to divide the spoil with the proud.*

Humility breaks the spirit of pride, and allows for us to receive truth. Notice in John 18:37, 38 how Pontius Pilate relates to Jesus by first asking Him the question, "What is truth? *...Pilate therefore said to Him, "Are You a king then?" Jesus answered, "You say rightly that I am a King. For this cause I was born, and for this cause I have come into the* *world, that I should bear witness to the truth, everyone who is of the truth hears My voice." Pilate said to Him, "What is truth?" And when he had said this, he went out again to the Jews, and said to them, "I find no fault in Him at all."*

Truth was able to penetrate Pontius Pilate's pride, thus allowing him to recognize the truth embodied in the one standing before him. May that same Spirit of Truth bless and guide you, so that you too will be able to say, "I find no fault in Him at all."

3

A Glimpse Into My Life

Since I was a young boy from the age of about five, I had a sense that something very special had been placed deep within my heart. I believe confirmation to that something special came in part early one summer when my older sisters and I, along with the other kids from our neighborhood were invited to come out to Vacation Bible School. In retrospect as I look back to that time, I have come to believe that "that something special" was a certain call on my life long before I was ever conceived in my mother's womb. At that young age, how could I describe or even express outwardly the changes I believed were taking place within my heart, and how could I have really known what a call was, or even by whom such a call could be given? Yet somehow I knew something very real and wonderful was taking place within my heart during that time.

I can still remember certain key blessings that I received in Vacation Bible School that particular summer. One of those blessings was found in a new song that we sang each day, as taught by our leaders. It was one of those new songs that instantly became my favorite. I would sing the chorus over and over again. Over the years I had forgotten the verses to that song, but I still could remember the chorus. The chorus went like this;

And He walks with me
And He talks with me
And He tells me I am His own
And the joy we share as we tarry there
None other has ever known

Recently as I was contemplating the significance of this chorus, I was re-introduced to that song, complete with all the verses.[2] God certainly has a wonderful way of bringing things together in His perfect timing, and for His ultimate purposes. The verses are as follows,

I come to the garden alone
While the dew is still on the roses
And the voice I hear falling on my ear
The Son of God discloses

He speaks and the sound of His voice
Is so sweet the birds hush their singing
And the melody that He gave to me
Within my heart is ringing

I'd stay in the garden with Him
Tho' the night around me be falling
But He bids go thro' the voice of woe
His voice to me is calling

As I look back to that time, I have come to believe that it was Holy Spirit preparing my heart to receive in stages, portions of the call that God had pre-ordained for me. It was the invitation of the promise found within the chorus of this song that my spirit was responding to.

Notice that in the last verse it says; ***"I'd stay in the garden with Him ... but He bids me go thro..."*** We are not to stay in the garden with the revelation of God's truth, but rather, we are to go out and share the good news, until the work is done. Then we may return to that special place, only to hear, "His voice on our ear falling..." again and again.

Over the years as the call on my life began taking shape (and it still is), it gradually became more defined through personal times of testing. It was through those personal times of testing that I tried shaking the call off my life, but instead the call became stronger and more refined. Since that time I have learned that I am not able to out run, out maneuver, or shake off God's plans and purposes that He has pre-ordained for me.

There are certain individuals called of God to be watchmen on the wall (intercessors/prayer warriors). They have been given discernment by Holy Spirit to know the seasons of time that we are in. These watchmen have the responsibility of praying God's Holy Word over the nations, governments, and specific territory. They also at times give specific warnings from Scripture of pending judgment for unrepentant acts of rebellion, disobedience, and for crimes against humanity. Warnings are given so that there may be opportunity for personal and corporate repentance.

I however, have been called specifically to be an ambassador of Jesus Christ and a minister of the Gospel bringing a glorious salvation message of hope, reconciliation, and restoration to the world, through the truth of God's Holy Word. Working in conjunction with the watchmen, the message of reconciliation and restoration can begin to do its work, once the need for genuine repentance is understood.

The call I believe that is on my life can best be summarized with the Scripture passage presented below. It was given to me by my pastor when I made a public profession of my faith at the age of about eighteen, approximately thirty five years ago.God certainly has a wonderful way of confirming the very things that He places in our hearts, confirming even those things that He placed in my heart at the age of five. *Now all things are of God, who has reconciled us to Himself through Jesus Christ, and has given us the ministry of reconciliation, that is, that God was in Christ, reconciling the world to Himself, not imputing their trespasses to them, and has committed to us the word of reconciliation. Now then, we are ambassadors for Christ, as though God were pleading through us; we implore (beg) you on Christ's behalf, be reconciled to God. For He made Him who knew no sin to be sin for us, that we might become the righteousness of God in Him.* 2 Corinthians 5:18–21.

4

The Mystery Man On
The Motorcycle

For eight summers previous to, and including the summer of 1996, a very kind man from my work allowed me, my wife Monika, and our five children–Robert, Leanne, Randall, David, and Sharlane the use of his cabin at Gun Lake. His cabin came complete with boat and motor, fishing gear, and motorcycle.

He never charged us any money for the use of his cabin. He and his wife just wanted to bless our family. I am sure that he realized raising a large family like ours prohibited us from affording such vacations otherwise. One of the most astonishing aspects concerning this man's generosity is that he trusted us completely with all of his personal belongings associated with his cabin.

I had a very special tradition with my children during our time at the cabin. I would take each child one at a time on a motorcycle ride up a very steep mountain trail to a spectacular lookout point high above Gun Lake. It would probably take a couple of hours to hike to the lookout point on foot, but on the motorcycle it could be done in approximately twenty five minutes.

There was only one trail leading up to the lookout point. Nearing the top of the mountain, the trail followed along a ridge with cliff on either side that eventually opened up to a small flat clearing among aged lodge pole pines. After arriving at the site, looking out in every direction you could see snow capped mountains, pine tree forested valleys and of course a pristine tranquil blue/green Gun Lake sparkling with dancing sunlight. The sky was nearly always cloudless and ever so blue. The added touch of a warm summer breeze made this special place complete. One of the most miraculous qualities about this place is the fact that the view was a never changing constant. In a rapidly changing world, the unchanging constant of Gun Lake brought great peace into the lives of my family.

Early one evening during the summer of 1996, it was time to start the annual pilgrimage of taking each child to the lookout for a picture and for a time of praise and thanksgiving. David, seven years old at the time, was the first to go. He was excited, and so was I. After fitting David with his safety helmet, away we went. Some parts of the trail were bumpy and very steep, but with the motorcycle engine wound flat out making lots of noise and creating a trail of blue smoke, we blazed our way up to the lookout point. With jerking handlebars, snapping tree branches and flying shrubs and bush, we didn't have a care in the world. We were in our element. Eventually we made it to the top, glowing red hot exhaust pipe and all!

While reaching to turn off the ignition, to my disbelief, the ignition key was gone. The engine was still running because the ignition switch was in the contact position. Somewhere along the trail we lost the key, probably due to the fact that the terrain was very rough. Perhaps engine vibration caused the key to jiggle out of its position. Who knows?

Panic began to grip me because of the fact that we were in grizzly bear country! Not only that, it was approximately 6 p.m. Early evening was setting in. I was afraid that if by chance the engine conked out, I would not be able to restart it. We were a couple of hours on foot away from safety. I did not want to meet any bears that evening, knowing they were around because of the posted warning signs and by our observation of fresh bear droppings along parts of the trail.

Many thoughts were racing though my mind upon our immediate arrival to the lookout point. Just then, and literally within seconds of our arrival, a man on a motorcycle appeared, or so it seemed. He pulled right up alongside of us. He could not have been following behind us, otherwise I would have spotted him through my rear view mirrors, and David and I certainly did not hear the rev's of his motorcycle engine. There was only one trail leading up to where we were, with not another person in sight for miles around. His sudden appearance startled us, to say the very least. This encounter would become even stranger as events began to unfold.

In my awkward bewilderment, I managed to ask the mystery man a rather dumb question. *"Isn't the view up here beautiful?"* He just looked at us, not once glancing over toward the view. He responded by saying; *"Yes, it certainly is!"* How strange I thought. He then said how amazed he was that the two of us made it all the way up to the lookout point on such a small motorcycle. I explained to him about our family tradition of coming to this place, but left out the part of giving praise and thanksgiving to God. I certainly was not a very good witness!

I began telling him about losing our motorcycle key. Looking over toward our motorcycle ignition switch he said; *"Yes, I can see that indeed you have!"* While drawing our attention over toward his ignition switch system he said; *"My keys are secure. I cannot lose them!"* Pointing toward his key, he showed us that his key was secured to the handlebars of his motorcycle with a long black plastic zap strap. (A type of strap electricians us for bunching wires together). I was really impressed with his simple and yet totally effective method of securing his motorcycle keys.

All I could think about was how I was going to explain the loss of my motorcycle key to the man who allowed us the use of his cabin. His motorcycle was an older model Yamaha. I'd probably have to buy a whole new ignition switch assembly, complete with new keys. It would probably have to be back-ordered from who knows where, none would be available, because of the age of the motorcycle, etc, etc... You know the story. Oh such worry! All I could think of, was the replacement dollar cost.

The mystery man on the motorcycle was speaking very prophetically concerning the security of keys. I knew within my spirit I needed to take heed to what was just shared with us concerning the security of keys.

He then asked us if we would be all right, reminding us of the fact that we were in active grizzly bear country. Realizing that our ignition switch was still on, whatever fear I had, was dissipating. If the engine stalled (it was running all this time), I could in theory kick-start the engine. I answered him by saying that we would be just fine. Then he said; ***"Good, I'll be seeing you then!"*** He turned his motorcycle around and proceeded to ride back down the trail that he supposedly had just come up only moments before.

Immediately I stalled out our motorcycle. David and I watched the mystery man ride down the trail until he was out of sight. I put down our motorcycle, and walked over to the cliff edge with my son David. We were hoping at some point to catch a glimpse of him on one of the trail switchbacks. We did not once see his descent or hear the rev's of his engine! It was as if he just disappeared, not even being on the mountain at all!

David and I carried on with our yearly tradition of praising and thanking the Lord while taking in the spectacular view, even though I was still very upset about losing the key. David said; ***"Don't worry dad, we'll just pray about it! Maybe we'll find the motorcycle key on the way down!"*** We never did. I was convinced that it was gone forever. Before starting our ride off the mountain, I gave David a brand new camp jack knife. I took a picture of him with his new treasure, capturing the moment for a later time of remembrance.

The other children were patiently waiting for their turn on the motorcycle. When we finally arrived back to the cabin, David jumped off the motorcycle while I was still in the process of parking it under the same tree that I had done so many times before. He bolted straight into the cabin so that he could tell his mom the big story.

The next day was routine summer fun for the kids, and work for us. I could not get the mystery man out of my mind, or the prophetic significance concerning the fact that his keys were secure and how I was able to lose my keys because they were not secure. What could all of this mean?

Early the next morning I had a disturbing dream. As hard as I tried, I could not interpret the significance of its meaning. Monika, my wife reassured me that in due time the understanding would come.

5

The Dream

I dreamed that I was working on the nightshift with one of our maintenance men. It was about 6:15 a.m.–nearing the end of our shift. We were just starting to put his tools away when suddenly he stopped what he was doing, and began clutching his chest. Gasping for breath, he immediately became very pale, then ashen grey! At once I recognized this as an extreme medical emergency. I called for help to one of my co-workers. By this time, the distressed man had passed out. Quickly I laid him into the supine position placing my ear against his chest while feeling for a pulse! The other co-worker was very slow to respond, with no sense of urgency what so ever. He slowly walked over toward the first aid room to get the oxygen as I had requested. It seemed like hours before he made his way back to me and the dying man. When he finally did arrive, he did not stay to help. I positioned the oxygen mask over the face of the distressed man and began administering the oxygen. It was not helping. I didn't know what to do. I felt completely helpless. My co-worker friend was dying.

People began to gather around as they were preparing to start their shift. They just stood together in total silence with their hands in their pockets. I called out again to the other maintenance man so that he could call for an ambulance. Again, he was slow to respond. A few moments later he came back to me saying in super slow motion; *"Ambulance is on the way!"* Oddly he did not stay to help. The dying man was now in a deep unconscious state. What more could I do?

Just then the ambulance attendants arrived with all of their special life saving equipment. I was so relieved! The attendants brushed the crowd aside and made their way to the dying man. They removed his oxygen mask and just when I thought they were going to revive him, they stopped what they were doing. To my shock and horror they began to mock and ridicule me in front of everyone standing around. It was at this point that I woke up from my dream. I never did find out in my dream if the dying man was ever revived, or if the ambulance attendants brought him to the hospital.

After breakfast I just wanted to get away for awhile. Monika suggested that I go for a motorcycle ride. On my way over to the motorcycle, I spotted something lying on the ground beneath the motorcycle. It was a brand new black plastic strap just like the one the mystery man had attached to his motorcycle. How did that black plastic strap just happen to find its way to that spot? Who could have put it there? When, and why? I was beginning to feel a tremendous excitement in my spirit. I thanked the Lord while putting the plastic strap into my pocket for safe keeping. Somehow I knew that I would find my motorcycle key, and the interpretation of my dream!

While kick-starting the motorcycle engine, I said a little prayer that went something like this; *"Dear Lord, give me eyes of faith to see, so that I will be able to find the missing key, and ears to hear what You may say to me about my dream!"* Ever so carefully I began my slow journey of retracing our path from the day before. Finally I came to the most difficult part of the trail just as I was becoming the most discouraged. Suddenly I spotted something shiny glittering in the morning sun. Right in the center of the trail the missing key presented itself. I didn't know if I should laugh or cry! How did that key just happen to show up after two days of being lost? I put the key into my pocket alongside the black plastic strap for safe keeping. The motorcycle was running very nicely without the key anyway. I was determined to ride the rest of the way to the top of the mountain hoping to find the answers to my perplexing questions.

When I arrived at the lookout point, I parked the motorcycle and found a big old pine tree to sit under. I then shouted out to the Lord saying; *"Lord, I'm not coming off this mountain until You interpret the meaning of my dream, and the significance of the mystery mans secure keys!"*

It seemed like I had been resting for hours, but in reality it may have been only moments. Slowly the Lord began to speak deeply into the center of my understanding. It was not an audible voice, but yet there was no mistaking that it was indeed the voice of the Lord! This is what He shared with me.

"My son, you have asked Me about the keys. I shall tell you. Keys are very important, for they have many uses. They can be used for the purpose of securing (to close/lock-up), or they can be used for the purpose of setting free (to open/unlock). They can be used to change impossibilities into ways of possibilities. But most importantly, when My keys are placed into the hands of discerning individuals, those keys can be used to set the spiritual captives (prisoners) free. And so it is with My written Word. My Word is sharper than any two-edged sword. My Words are living keys. You my son, have been given living keys that can bring life or death! You must not lose them. The keys that I have given to you need to be so secure in your life that you will be able to use them when ever needed!"

I felt pierced through my soul, for I knew that I was not using the keys of Holy Scripture as I should. I knew there were times I had even lost the Word of God, because His Word was not buried deep within my heart like precious treasure. I remembered how much fun David and I were having motorcycling up the mountain just two days earlier. We were in our element and in our own little world. We were having such fun. Why would we be even thinking about keys anyway?I was afraid to ask the lord my next question, but I knew that I must. *"Lord, what about the dying man in my dream?"* The

Lord answered, *"My son, the dying man in your dream repre-sents humanity that seems to be perishing without any hope."* Again I felt pierced through my soul as I was being convicted by Holy Spirit. I asked the next question. *"Lord, who were all those people standing around with their hands in their pockets watching in silence?"* The lord answered, *"Those people call themselves Christians, but in reality they only have a form of godliness and no power what so ever. They cannot enter in, because they are blind."* I responded, *"But Lord, there are so many!"* The Lord said, *"Yes my son, and so it is!"* I asked my next question; *"Lord, who were the ambu-lance attendants?"* The Lord's next answer came as a total shock to me. He said; *"My son, the ambulance attendants in your dream are the modern day Sadducees and Pharisees*(the controlling religious leaders in biblical times).*They are the false prophets, the blind religious leaders, and the wicked shepherds who feed themselves, and not the flock! They are the accusers of your brethren, and they are evil backbiters and gossipers. They have no desire to enter into My truth and they prevent those that truly desire to enter in from doing so!"* I asked the Lord why they took off the oxygen mask from the face of the dying man, and why did they humiliate and mock me in front of those that were gathered around? The lord answered; *"My son, so they could bring exposure to the fact that you were failing to use the correct first aid tech-niques."* (Isn't that so true? We choose to bring exposure to one another's faults, rather than bring gentle correction and forgiveness. However, I do believe in bringing exposure to deliberate unrepentant acts of sin in the household of faith, so that it can be rooted out and be effectively taken care of. In fact Jesus Christ taught the correct procedure for this in Matthew 18:15-17. Please look this passage up for yourself. It is very important). *"My son, you had the right ideas. You called for help, you applied the oxygen, and then you called for the ambulance, but what you failed to do was to clear the dying mans obstructed airway and to keep it clear! All the oxygen in My creation could not save him. You did not have the keys of wisdom and knowledge in your possession!"*

The revelation of truth that was given to me that morning was absolutely overwhelming. I thanked the Lord for the very special encounter He had arranged for me as I excitedly made my way back to the cabin. Monika was smiling as I met up with her. With her gentle touch on my shoulder she said to me; *"I know that you are going to tell me that you have found your motorcycle key and that you have the interpretation of your dream!"* Somehow she knew all along in her spirit that I would.

Having the black plastic strap in my possession became one of my most prized souvenirs. The motorcycle was working just fine without the key anyway, so I put the key and the black plastic strap in one of the cabin drawers for safe keeping.

6

Wanting To Impress

A few weeks later, I was back at work on the afternoon shift. I had my souvenir black plastic zap strap in my pocket just waiting to tell the big story to a certain non-Christian co-worker. When the opportunity arose, I was able to tell him everything about my experience, as he listened in complete silence. When I finished my testimony, he wanted to review all of the events that I had shared with him.

He started with his first question; *"So, when you found the black plastic strap underneath the motorcycle you put it into your pocket? Now you are halfway up the trail and you find the motorcycle key. So you put it into your pocket alongside the plastic strap for safe keeping. Is that correct?"* I answered him by saying; *"Yes that is what I did!"* He then began rebuking me for not immediately attaching the key with the black plastic strap to the handle bars of the motorcycle. *"You didn't seem to learn a thing about what your "God" was teaching you! Even the mystery man spoke to you about his keys being secured. He even demonstrated this fact to you. But you sure didn't listen did you? All you could think about was your so-called testimony and furthermore, you put the key for the motorcycle in a drawer for safekeeping. That is just what I don't understand about you Christians. You claim to have the keys, but you put the Bible (living keys) in a drawer, afraid to share those words with anyone, because you want to keep them safe. Well, you can keep your religion as well!"*

Wow! If the stones within the ground could cry out! Was I ever put in my place! I told him that he had no idea what further revelation he had given me, and how he was used of God to teach me further truth. His anger toward me didn't last long. During his lunch break he went to Dairy Queen and bought two giant D.Q. blizzard treats that he brought back with him for us to enjoy together. I was very thankful for that precious moment with him.

7

The White Stone

... "Anyone who is willing to hear should listen to the Spirit and understand what the Spirit is saying to the churches. Everyone who is victorious will eat of the manna that has been hidden away in Heaven. And I will give to each one a white stone, and on the stone will be engraved a new name that no one knows except the one who receives it. Revelation 2:17 NLT.

Often times I have wondered what God had in mind regarding the giving of a new name written on white stone as recorded in Revelation 2:17. Deep within my soul I have longed to understand the significance of receiving such a fine gift. One day, the answer to my prayer regarding the white stone and the new name that is written upon it came to me through a dream.

Although it is my desire to share with you what has been revealed to me concerning our new name that is written on white stone, we must not overlook the importance of what it means to be an over-comer as stated in the first part of verse 17 of Revelation Chapter 2. Overcoming starts with heartfelt repentance. Jesus Christ paid the ultimate price for our restoration back to God our Creator by way of His reconciliatory work, becoming the perfect sacrifice for our sin according to

God's eternal purpose. His sacrifice made a way possible for every person, to become a son or daughter of the Most High. According to Philippians 2:12, all those who become sons and daughters of the Most High are called to work out their salvation with fear and trembling. This can only be done with true saving faith that always starts with repentance! True saving faith is a gift from God that allows for His grace to help us begin this work.

As we begin to grow in faith, maturity, wisdom and responsibility, we will find ourselves stepping back into the garden of the Lord. The Kingdom of God, then begins to manifest its reality through us in time and space. While it is yet day we have the opportunity to become a part of that great company that will rule and reign in the ages to come with Jesus the Christ.

At the precise moment that we are able to understand the profound significance of Christ's sacrifice for each of us personally by faith, (faith comes by hearing the gospel of Jesus the Christ. Jesus Christ is the narrow gate) our salvation is activated. This is what is meant when we are born again of the spirit. If we come under the Lordship of Jesus Christ and submit our will to His will, He then begins to transform us individually into His image over time. As our mind is being renewed from the carnal nature of our sinful existence and from the ways of the world, by His power and with the help of Holy Spirit, we become sons and daughters of the living God. This amazing process brings us into a loving relationship with Him.

Through disobedience, Adam and Eve lost the Light (God's glory) that they were immersed in. The Light of God's glory was their covering. Infinite love from the very heart of God, made a way possible for the Light to be restored to Adam and Eve, and to each of us as well. If we are to be a carrier and a reflector of God's glory now, and in the eternal ages to come, it will be through sonship. Our inheritance from God our Father is the re-establishment of His glory in our personal lives. This inheritance is for His family members. Sonship establishes us as heirs through his Son Jesus Christ the Lamb of God.

Salvation was made available for every person before they were conceived in their mother's womb, whether physically born into this world or not. This salvation was established by God from the foundation of the world. However, it is necessary for our salvation to be activated by faith in order for us to begin to understand its ultimate purpose in our life! Sin enslaves us to the dragon (Satan). *All who dwell on the earth will worship him, [the dragon] whose names have not been written in the Book Of Life of the Lamb slain from the foundation of the world* Revelation 13:8.

Thank God for His grace and mercy when He brings us out from the Kingdom of Darkness and into the Kingdom of His wonderful Light. At the precise moment of each person's restoration, their name will be added into the Lambs Book of Life. It is to be noted that Scripture reveals that many names are also pre-recorded in the Lambs Book of Life. Everything that God does is always in His perfect timing. He exists outside the dimension of time and space as we know it, thus making it difficult, but not impossible for us to understand His ways.

When we renounce the works of Satan from our lives, we will be rewarded with the works of Christ that will begin to manifest outwardly from our regenerated lives over time! These are the hidden works (free gifts of grace) that God has prepared before hand for us. Any works that we produce in the flesh (self effort) outside of Christ will be burned away like wood, straw and stubble. Everlasting rewards that will never fade are works of gold, silver, and precious stones (more on this later).

Every believer within the Body of Christ (fellowship of the saints), has been given the opportunity to be a bright shining star (Light) in the glorious Kingdom of God. If however, we continue in our own effort and strength, like Adam and Eve, we too will have missed this blessing in more ways than one.

8

The Banqueting Table

Late one night while in a semi-dream state, I believe that I was caught up in the Spirit of the Lord. During that time He began sharing with me the significance of our eternal worth but equally as important, Holy Spirit began revealing to me God's personal thoughts He has for each of us through the following Scripture passages.

O Lord, you have examined my heart and know everything about me. You know when I sit down or stand up. You know my every thought when far away. You chart the path ahead of me and tell me where to stop and rest. Every moment You know where I am. You know what I am going to say even before I say it, Lord. You both precede and follow me. You place your hand of blessing on my head. Such knowledge is too wonderful for me, too great for me to know! I can never escape from Your spirit! I can never get away from Your presence! If I go up to Heaven, You are there; if I go down to the place of the dead, You are there. If I ride the wings of the morning, if I dwell by the farthest oceans, even there Your hand will guide me, and Your strength will support me. I could ask the darkness to hide me and the light around me to become night – but even in darkness I cannot hide from You. To You the night shines as bright as day. Darkness and light are both alike to You. You made all the delicate, inner parts of my body and knit me together in my mother's womb. Thank You for making me so wonderfully complex! Your workmanship is marvelous – and how well I know it. You saw me before I was born. Every day of my life was recorded in Your book. Every moment was laid out before a single day had passed. How precious are Your thoughts about me, O God! They are innumerable! I can't even count them; they outnumber the grains of sand! And when I wake up in the morning, You are still with me! Psalm 139:1-18 NLT.

It is God who saved us and chose us to live a Holy life. He did this not because we deserved it, but because that was His plan long before the world began – to show His love and kindness to us through Christ Jesus. And now He has made all of this plain to us by the coming of Christ Jesus, our Savior, who broke the power of death and showed us the way to everlasting life through the Good News. 2 Timothy 1:9, 10 NLT.

God has made everything beautiful for its own time. He has planted eternity in the human heart, but even so, people cannot see the whole scope of God's work from beginning to end. Ecclesiastes 3:11 NLT. *Everything has already been decided. It was known long ago what each person would be. So there's no use arguing with God about your destiny.* Ecclesiastes 6:10 NLT. *We may throw the dice, but the Lord determines how they fall.* Proverbs 16:33 NLT. *You can make many plans, but the Lord's purpose will prevail.* Proverbs 19:21 NLT. *For then the dust will return to the earth, and the spirit will return to God who gave it.* Ecclesiastes 12:7 NLT. *Yet what we suffer now is nothing compared to the glory He will give us later. For all creation is waiting eagerly for that future day when God will reveal who His children really are. Against its will, all of creation was subjected to God's curse. But with eager hope, the creation looks forward to the day when it will join God's children in glorious freedom from death and decay. For we know that all creation has been groaning as in the pains of childbirth right up to the present time. And we believers also groan, even though we have the Holy Spirit within us as a foretaste of future glory, for we long for our bodies to be released from sin and suffering. We, too, wait with eager hope for the day when God will give us our full rights as His adopted children, including the new bodies He has promised us. We were given this hope when we were saved. If we already have something, we don't need to hope for it. Now that we are saved, we eagerly look forward to this freedom. For if you already have something, you don't need to hope for it. But if we look forward to something we don't yet have, we must wait patiently and confidently.* Romans 8:18-25 NLT.

As I was contemplating the importance of these Scripture passages, unexpectedly I was swiftly transported to a distant place. Soon I found myself to be among a vast mixed multitude of people. We were standing in front of two massive hand crafted wooden doors that were beautifully engraved with incredibly detailed designs and sacred inscriptions describing heavenly things.

Suddenly there was a sound of many trumpets. At that precise moment, the doors began to open inwardly, revealing an enormous hall of grand cathedral-like proportions. Spiritual beings like angels were standing at attention, side by side in complete silence all along the interior perimeter walls of this magnificent hall. They each had in their possession a beautiful silver trumpet.

I was greeted with great enthusiasm by a finely dressed person that knew me by my first name. This person explained to me that I had been invited along with countless others to a very special banqueting celebration. As my name was being checked off from the guest list, I was ushered to a very special place at the most lavishly decorated banqueting table that anyone could possibly imagine. Although the banqueting table was stretched out in length as far as my eyes could see, in my spirit I knew that there was a place reserved just for me! Immediately I could identify with my place setting by the very chair that was fashioned exclusively for me. Because no two chairs were exactly alike, there was no desire or need to jostle for the position of the favored right-hand seat. The banqueting table was able to accommodate every single person in such a way that each seat that was customized specifically for that person appeared to be the favored right-hand seat. How amazing!

Note: The context for the favored right-hand seat is referenced in Matthew 20: 20-23. ... *Then the mother of Zebedee's sons came to Him with her sons, kneeling down and asking something from Him. And He said to her, "What do you wish?" She said to Him, "Grant that these two sons of mine may sit, one on Your right hand and the other on the left, in Your kingdom." But Jesus answered and said, "You do not know what you ask. Are you able to drink the cup that I am about to drink, and be baptized with the baptism that I am baptized with?" They said to Him, "We are able." So He said to them, "You will indeed drink My cup, and be baptized with the baptism that I am baptized with; but to sit on My right hand and on My left is not Mine to give, but it is for those for whom it is prepared by My Father."*

Each chair was lovingly handcrafted for the individual that would be seated there. The chair that was fashioned for me was a perfect form fit, right down to the armrests. The quality of workmanship was remarkable. The materials, the special engravings and unique carvings spoke profoundly of the great care and attention to the exacting detail that was given to such magnificent creations. As I looked on, immediately I could sense the incredible love that was crafted into these wonderful gifts. As each person took their position in their exclusively personalized chair, life transforming ministry of pure love began to be administered to each person directly from Father God's heart!

None of us could see Father God directly at this point due to the intensity of pure white light that was being emitted from the very essence of His being. Somehow I knew within my spirit that this gradually would change, and that eventually we would all be able to see Him in His fullness, face to face, and spirit to Spirit.

Wave after wave of rippling love was pouring into our

souls, causing us to sink more deeply into the perfect form of our chairs. As we were all being ministered to, I noticed that every place setting was different. My place setting was intricately detailed with patterns of inlayed silver and highlighted with golden hughes of autumn color and made from materials that I could naturally identify with. No two goblets were the same. Each goblet was crafted from materials specific to the likes of the individual including style, shape, size and weight. Another amazing detail not to be overlooked was that each goblet was form fit perfectly to each person's hand. Also the very essence of the drink contained within each goblet was a distinctive blend of taste and variation specifically hand crafted for the enjoyment and benefit of each individual.

Again, wave after wave of healing love from Father God's heart was being poured into our souls as we began to appreciate more deeply the personalized detail of our individual place settings. As I sipped the golden nectar from my goblet, Father God spoke ever so lovingly to me. He told me that even when I was in my deepest pain and hurt as a young child, He had not forgotten me!

As He spoke, ripples of warmth and healing love began transforming me from the present glorious moment into the next. Abba Father continued by saying that every aspect of the banqueting table was lovingly prepared before the foundation of the world for the purpose of bringing healing and restoration for those moments in each of our lives when we felt to be the most lonely, vulnerable, abandoned, rejected, or forsaken. Not only were the emblems fashioned by His hand contained within the experience of the banqueting table as previously mentioned for healing, they also hallmarked times of celebration and victorious moments of achievement in each of our lives, and especially those moments that may have gone by un-noticed by those whom should have noticed the most.

Father God also revealed to me through the emblems of the banqueting meal that not one thought, word, or deed, pain, sorrow, or joy, experience–good, bad, or ugly, was ever wasted in any of our lives. Every aspect of every detail in our

God given life is always redeemable and for the benefit of our character development.

The pain from the atrocities of evil that permeate throughout the earth staggers and boggles the human mind. Who can comprehend the benefit of such insanity? Crusades, inquisitions, pogroms, holocausts, genocide, murder, abortion, torture, war, starvation, terrorism, homicide bombings, upheaval, rape, molestation, pestilence, disease, despair, loneliness, hopelessness, wasted lives and endless suffering. I asked Father God where was He in all of this madness? Again He answered by saying that He is always in perfect control, and that His hands are never tied by the conditions of this world or our personal circumstances.

While in our earthly existence, we have been given the opportunity to either administer love, or receive love, to give mercy, or receive mercy, to forgive, or be forgiven, to give a cup of cold water to those who thirst, or receive that same cup. Every day we are given the choice to embrace ethnic diversity, or repel it, to reason with one another, or fight with one another. Each new day given is filled with opportunity for us to prefer, encourage, build up, promote, and bless one another. There really are no limits as to what can be accomplished when we discipline and bring our self directed wills into the submission of God's eternal purpose.

I was beginning to understand and see more clearly for the first time, that all of the interactions that we have ever experienced in our earthly lives are by God's design and for His glorious eternal purpose and too numerous for us to count.

After what seemed to be an eternity of incredible warmth, love and healing grace from Father God, to everyone's delight, the main course of the banqueting meal was being served. Again, no two meals were alike. Every meal was lovingly prepared by Father God Himself and seasoned perfectly to the inimitable taste of each person! As we consumed our meals, great conversations were beginning to take place.

It was wonderfully strange that countless conversations could take place simultaneously without chaos or confusion.

It didn't seem to matter where a person sat at the banqueting table, you could converse with any person of your choosing in perfect peace and harmony as if you were face to face with that person. There were literally billions of conversations taking place simultaneously, much to the pleasure of Father God as He looked on!

To complement the gala festivities, every delectable desert imaginable was spread out on pure white linen for all to enjoy. Somehow I knew in my spirit that every person that was invited to be present at the banqueting table was accounted for. Not one person was missing.

Suddenly, and without prior notice, the spiritual beings that were still standing at attention in their original positions raised their silver trumpets to their lips and sounded in perfect unison a series of trumpet blasts that ranged in varying degrees of intensity and dimension. Immediately there was a hushed silence as everyone looked on.

After several long moments of silence, I could see two doors begin to open. Immediately everyone stood to their feet giving full attention to the person about to enter the dining hall. It was the honored host, the master of ceremonies!

I could not look directly upon the face of this individual for several moments, but it was very evident to all that this person was none other than Jesus the Christ, our Kinsmen Redeemer. He was very gracious and loving. There was incredible warmth radiating outwardly from His smile that was absolutely glorious! As He gazed upon all who stood in His presence, once again, wave after wave of rippling love was pouring into our souls. To finally come face to face with "the Lamb of God who takes away the sin of the world" was absolutely exhilarating! Words cannot begin to describe the absolute beauty of this life transforming moment, and the Holy sacredness of the next series of events to follow.

Yeshua (the Hebrew name for Jesus) was holding in His arms a large silver platter that contained perfectly arranged piles of small white stones with inscriptions written in gold on each one.

Without delay, Yeshua began to minister to each person individually. During this ministry time, there was a hushed silence, reverence, and respect for the one being ministered to. Time was no longer a restraining factor whilst each person awaited their turn for personal ministry.

In my observations, I could see Yeshua approach an individual without speaking a word. He would look ever so tenderly into the eyes of the one being ministered to and then begin to speak to that person Spirit to spirit. Every question, need, concern– whether for a healing, deliverance or whatever, was dealt with and corrected immediately. Every crooked path within the life of the person being ministered to was made straight. Yeshua was able to break every yoke of bondage and take that person from the present glorious moment to the next!

Each person had their life reviewed without any everlasting negative judgment or consequence. Whatever judgments that may have been necessary, were always for corrective eternal purposes. Yeshua's primary objective for this ministry time was always for full restoration, and for the administering of His Father's grace and mercy. He was completing the perfecting of His Bride so that she would be free from any spot or wrinkle. The Bride of Christ, a living Church, not a building, was being prepared to become image bearers, and reflectors of God's glory throughout the eternal ages to come!

When the person that was being ministered to was fully satisfied that all of his or her questions or concerns were addressed, and when it was confirmed in their spirit that the work of reconciliation and restoration was complete, it was then at that time I could see Yeshua take a carefully selected white stone from the silver platter and place it ever so gently into the hand of the one to whom it was meant to be given.

What the Lord allowed me to see next was absolutely astounding. As each person took his or her white stone during their personal time of ministry with the Lord and began to read their new name that was found to be written upon it, immediately they were able to comprehend the meaning of their new name!

The meaning of our new name is actually a highly detailed blueprint of our spiritual D.N.A. Deep within our spiritual D.N.A. is embedded the essence of the person we were really created to be, long before we were ever knit in our mother's womb! *...For all creation is waiting eagerly for that future day when God will reveal who His children really are.* Romans 8:19 NLT. *...For you died when Christ died, and your real life is hidden with Christ in God. And when Christ, who is your real life, is revealed to the whole world, you will share in all His glory.* Colossians 3:3, 4 NLT.

In our earthly life, we have been conditioned to jump through many hoops of religious performance and tradition that in reality will not count for anything in the grand scheme of things. The things that will be blessed and rewarded are the things that Father God in His sovereignty pre-determined for us beforehand. God is gracious, and loving, keeping our best interests close to His heart.

We are being prepared for our eternal destiny based upon the finished works of Christ that were hidden in our D.N.A. long before the foundation of the world. It was shown to me that the measure of every reward given or taken is perfectly matched to the individual by Father God's pre-determination including every degree of glory, rank, or position. Each given gift is perfectly just, right and fitting!

Crowns of gold, silver, and precious stones were also awarded to individuals for unselfish acts of service. Later, at a predetermined time, the very crowns that were given out as rewards were cast down at the feet of Jesus the Christ in honor of Him.

As each person gazed upon the beauty of the "Living Christ" in His entire majestic splendor, He slowly raised the first of two cups that were set before Him, reserved precisely for this moment. The first cup raised was "The Cup of Redemption," in commemoration of His death. We were all invited to partake with our Lord in this cup!

...He has delivered us from the power of darkness and conveyed us into the kingdom of the Son of His love, in whom

we have redemption through His blood, the forgiveness of sins. He is the image of the invisible God, the firstborn over all creation. For by Him all things were created that are in Heaven and that are on earth, visible and invisible, whether thrones or dominions or principalities or powers. All things were created through Him and for Him. And He is before all things, and in Him all things consist. And He is the head of the body, the church, who is the beginning, the firstborn from the dead, that in all things He may have the preeminence. For it pleased the Father that in Him all the fullness should dwell, and by Him to reconcile all things to Himself, by Him, whether things on earth or things in Heaven, having made peace through the blood of His cross. And you, who once were alienated and enemies in your mind by wicked works, yet now He has reconciled in the body of His flesh through death, to present you holy, and blameless, and above reproach in His sight. Colossians 1:13-22.

The second cup that was placed before Him, called "The Cup of Praise" (the fourth cup as found in the Jewish Seder), was the cup that He said He would not drink from again until the day it would be drank anew in His Fathers Kingdom! (Matthew 26:29). I had a deep sense within my spirit that this cup was reserved for a special time forthcoming where there will be a final settling of all things. This final "settling" will take place at the "Marriage Supper Of The Lamb!"

After sharing in "The Cup of Redemption," Yeshua led the way to a passage that brought us all outside of the grand banqueting hall. Once outside, we could see a beautiful river of living water flowing from the very throne of God. We were led single file through this river until we were fully immersed in its warmth. A final cleansing took place through this indescribable process. As we emerged from these living waters, one by one, each person placed their white stone down in such a way that an alter of stones began to be built as a monument of thanks-giving. In an amazing, wonderfully strange way, there were countless others coming from another direction that also had white stones. They joined in the building of the monument of thanks-giving. From this point, we were all ushered into a beautiful garden. In the center of this garden was planted a very special tree; ...*"He who has an ear, let him hear what the Spirit says to the churches. To him who overcomes I will give to eat from the tree of life, which is in the midst of the Paradise of God."* Revelation 2:7.

As my time with the Lord was concluding, I could see those within the garden partaking freely of the fruit from "The Tree of Life." As they partook, immediately those persons began zooming off in all directions at lightning speed into the things that were prepared for them in advance and in accordance with their new name that was written on white stone, all to the glory of Father God, His Son, and Holy Spirit. Hallelujah, praise the Lord! Amen.

9

Pre-Eminent Glory Of The Lord

L ate one night while in a semi-dream state, I believe I was caught up in the Spirit of the Lord. It seemed like my spirit was literally being carried away by the Lord to what appeared to be a vast open area. Filling this area as far as my eyes could see was a countless mass of humanity that appeared to be waiting with great expectation for some type of an event to occur. Immediately following this observation, I found myself to be standing with a group of several hundred other Christians on a hill overlooking this great mixed multitude.

As we stood there gazing in silence, we slowly raised outstretched arms over this enormous audience and began shouting out blessings that were filled with promises from the Lord that included prophetic declarations and proclamations. While in this state, I could hear that we were shouting such things as; *"Father God has forgiven you through His Son Jesus the Christ, He no longer is holding your sins against you, for He has taken the sins of your past and thrown them into the sea of His forgetfulness, He longs to commune and fellowship with you and desires to wipe all of your tears away. Come! For the Lord in His unfailing love has made ready a banqueting table prepared for you!"*

As we were concluding our proclamations, suddenly

there was an ear piercing blast from a trumpet (shofar horn) that sounded like a mighty rushing wind. Resonating sound waves rippled through us and our audience at lightning speed. The power from these reverberations immediately caused every person to fall to the ground like dead men. The heavens began to open, filling every square inch of the sky with the pre-eminent glory of Jesus Christ. As His pre-eminent glory began to fall, I could see a Holy awe and reverence come over every single person including myself. As this was happening, life sustaining breath was being drawn out from each individual as we all began pressing our faces into the dirt while covering the back of our heads with our hands!

Immediately I found myself back in my bed fully awake and literally gasping for my very breath. As I became re-orientated to my natural surroundings, I realized that I had experienced what apparently was a very real supernatural encounter.

I glanced over to Monika my wife, who was still sleeping soundly. She had no idea of what I had just experienced. It took several days before I was able to share this event with her and many months later before I could share this event with anyone else. Since that remarkable experience, I have come to firmly believe that God's heart is for all of humanity as represented in that great mixed multitude.

10

A Covenant Made Between A Jew And A Gentile

Many pages could be filled if I were to share with you every amazing detail regarding our first trip to Israel. So at this point I will only share with you a portion of a very special encounter Monika and I had with a young religious Jewish couple on that particular trip.

It was three o'clock a.m. on the morning of Shavuot (Pentecost) Sunday June 4th, 1995, in the old city of Jerusalem when we were woken from our sleep by the sound of hundreds of voices, the singing of songs in Hebrew, and the shuffling of feet in the street outside our bedroom window. We immediately dressed our selves, grabbed our video camera equipment and joined the steady stream of people that were heading down to the Western Wall, also known as the Wailing Wall or in the Hebrew language, the Kotel.

This pilgrimage to the Wailing Wall is an annual event that starts on the eve of Pentecost, a Jewish High Holy Day! Young and old alike stay up all night reading and reciting Holy Scripture, while others sing songs of deliverance and redemption. Also during this time of celebrating, thanksgiving is offered up to God for the giving of the law as found in the five books of Moses. In contrast, many Christians celebrate Pentecost as the time when Holy Spirit was given freely to the early followers (believers) of Jesus Christ. This event marked the time on the early Christian calendar for the traditional beginning of the Church age.

It was still dark outside as Monika and I and countless others made our way to the vast open plaza immediately in front of the Wailing Wall. Thousands of people filled every square inch of the plaza. Before anyone was allowed to enter the secured area of the plaza, we all had to pass through a check point set up by the I.D.F. (Israeli Defense Force). Security personnel were not permitting anyone with any type of camera or video equipment to pass through, including a film crew on assignment from Australia expecting to film a documentary on this Jewish High Holy Day. Monika and I just happened to be grouped with them. When it was our turn to pass through the check point, one of the Israeli soldiers asked me to show him the contents of my shoulder bag. I had no choice but to show him my video camera equipment. He hesitated for a moment while looking around and then quickly nodded us through including our video equipment–God's favor!

Once inside the secured area, we began our search for the perfect observation point. Within a few short moments we found an excellent vantage point high above the plaza on a grassy hill across from the Wailing Wall. The silhouette of the Mount of Olives made for a perfect backdrop contrasting the Wailing Wall as it glistened in silver moon light. I immediately began videotaping all of the proceedings. We were able to record once in a lifetime video footage, with some of the most remarkable film footage ever to be recorded by me! Young girls dressed in pretty party dresses, complete with matching white frilly socks and polished dress shoes, boys and young men in black suits with white shirts, long bearded old men wrapped in their prayer shawls (Talit) clutching prayer books while holding them close to their chests, mothers with babies in arm, and young ladies looking on. A sight to behold and a truly joyous occasion for all!

As I was video recording every possible moment of this panorama, suddenly from behind, I received a rather sharp tap on my left shoulder. Before I could turn off my video camera or even turn around to see who was tapping my shoulder, a very stern woman's voice in broken English told me to; *"Please turn off your camera. This is our High Holy Day! We find it very offensive for anyone to be taking pictures or to video record this special time!"*Monika and I immediately apologized to the young woman who was standing behind us with her young children.

I began telling her that we meant no harm, nor did we want to offend anyone. I explained that we were Christians from Canada with a great love for Israel and her people, and that we belonged to a prayer group in Canada that intercedes through prayer to God on behalf of Israel and her people. I also told her that we were praying for the safety of the Israeli army, their families and especially the young children.

The young woman began to weep softly as Monika and I shared these things with her. Suddenly the young woman's husband, who was standing off to her side, stepped in front of his wife–almost pushing her out of the way. He seemed to be very upset over the fact that as a Christian man I was even talking to his wife without his consent.Taking an authoritive position between his wife and us, the young woman's husband crossed his arms over his chest, and began to rapidly ask many questions concerning our faith and what our beliefs were. Before we could even answer any of his questions, he asked me a loaded question that I believe was his original intention all along. This is what he asked; *"So! Tell me about this Messiah of yours! Who do you think this man really is?"*Wow! What could I say? I was speechless, and completely taken off guard. I didn't know how to respond. I was standing in front of a religious Jew who was well versed in the Torah. There was no doubt whatsoever in my mind that he knew in advance of this complex question what the Holy Scriptures had to say about the Messiah. He could probably answer this question in a deeper Hebraic way than I ever could as a Gentile!

I offered up a quick prayer to God under my breath asking

Him for help in answering this question. After all, I certainly didn't want to offend this man with truth. God immediately answered my prayer by speaking directly into my heart. What He said was right to the point. *"My son, just tell him the truth about who I am!"*I was trembling as I acknowledged the Lord, telling Him that I would do as He said. Holy Spirit was already filling my mouth with words to speak. So in one deep breath and in one very long continuous sentence I blurted out; *"You asked me who I believe the Messiah is, I shall tell you. The Messiah is none other than Jesus the Christ who in all truth is God Himself manifest in the flesh as the perfect God man! God made Himself become the perfect sacrifice for our sin by being born of a virgin fully human in every way, but without sin. He became the ultimate sacrifice for you (Jew) and me (Gentile)."*

Wow! Did I just say all of that? The young man was outraged and visibly shaken. He was actually hostile to the things I had just blurted out, which is completely understandable! In response, this is what he said; *"How can you say this to me? How can you expect me to hear such blasphemy? Do you not understand that as a Jew we understand God to be only as one, according to Holy Scripture?"* I did not know how to respond to his comeback. I was no match for his in-depth knowledge of traditional Jewish thought regarding the Torah. How was I going to diffuse this volatile situation? At that precise moment Holy Spirit began speaking to my heart, telling me to just simply say; *"For now!"*Raising my hand over the young man, I simply said; *"For now!"*Instantly his demeanor changed from hostility to that of becoming completely undone (unarmed). He was now as gentle as a little lamb. Turning to his wife, I took the lapel pin of the red maple leaf of Canada that was pinned to my shirt and gave it to her. I told her to accept this small token as a reminder that there were Canadian Christians praying for Israel, the peace of Jerusalem and most importantly, the well being of Jewish families and all those serving in the I.D.F. What took place next was almost indescribable. The young man that was so hostile only moments before was now extending his right hand of fellowship to me.He was wearing a beautiful prayer shirt that his wife had made for Him. Traditional tassels (Tsitsit) were sewn onto the bottom hem on either side of the garment. The tassels were knotted in such a way as to be constant reminders to the person wearing the garment that each individual knot represented one of the commandments of the Lord concerning Jewish moral and religious conduct. Interwoven through each of the knots was a single blue thread, thus making the tassels, "tassels of greatness."Ironically, the blue thread is actually a symbolic prophetic representation of the Messianic promises concerning Jesus Christ the Messiah, yet to be discovered by the majority of the Jewish people. The person wearing the fringed (Tsitsit) garment just doesn't know it yet! I have no doubt believing that this prayer shirt was one of this man's most prized possessions.

The interactions that had just taken place on the grassy hill between Monika, myself and the young couple were in plain sight of thousands of Jewish people. Suddenly and unexpectantly, our new Jewish friend stripped off his prayer shirt right down to his bare back. He then carefully rolled his prayer shirt up and gave it to me as a gift. He said that today he was making a covenant with us (Monika and I). He wanted his prayer shirt to be a symbol of reconciliation, restoration and peace between Jew and Gentile. He further said that He believed that together Jew and Gentile would find salvation in the living Messiah of the Bible and that one day we would be as one. He spoke prophetically over us, saying that he believed Monika and I would be able to reach the Jewish people with a message of God's unfailing love in a very special way, going into certain places that he himself would be unable to go into himself.

Monika and I thanked him and his wife profusely for the sacred gift and for the profoundly important exchange of dialogue that had taken place. This was truly a divinely arranged appointment!

By this time, the early morning sun was just beginning to

rise over the Mount of Olives. I felt an unction in my spirit to begin video recording the sunrise. I quickly turned on my camera and began recording the most amazing event. As the sun began rising in majestic hues of gold and orange, it broke out in grand splendor over the top of the Wailing Wall. I was able to capture on film a very distinct single ray of golden-orange/white light begin to shimmer down onto the enormous crowd of people that filled every square inch of the plaza. Suddenly there was a second and then a third distinct ray of golden-orange white/light that totally flooded the plaza covering every person like a blanket. Holy Spirit impressed upon me in a non audible way that Father God had not forgotten His ancient covenant people, and that all of His promises concerning them would be realized. The three rays of golden-orange/white light were a graphic representation of Father, Son, and Holy Spirit.

Reminiscing back to the time when the young Jewish man spoke prophetically over us in 1995, I began realizing to a large degree what he had prophesied in many ways had already come to pass for us in 1997 and then again in 2011. We indeed have gone into some of the very places that he knew as a religious Jew, he could never get to himself. I will share the events of 2011 in the next chapter.

By divine arrangement, in the summer of 1997, Monika and I joined a small ministry team from Christian Friends of Israel on a journey that led us to holocaust survivors and their families in the Ukraine. Our team was able to locate many Jewish families desiring to make Aliyah (Jewish emigration) to Israel. We ministered God's unconditional love and emotional healing to many of the elderly whom we met, while contributing the necessary finances that would eventually pay the way for approximately 450 families to make their dreams and prayers for Aliyah come true.

This miracle was made possible by the hand of God through intercessory prayer and with international monetary donations collected in advance by an amazing network of Christian Zionists. We also had the privilege of escorting these Jewish immigrants by chartered ship from Odessa over the Black Sea, the Sea of Marmara, the Mediterranean Sea and then onto the sea port city of Haifa Israel.

This particular voyage was accomplished through the international ministry of "Operation Exodus Ebenezer Emergency Fund" in partnership with "Christian Friends of Israel." Much could be said about this trip, perhaps in a future writing. God is a covenant keeper. His heart is very much for the total restoration and reconciliation of not only the Jewish people, but ultimately every people group, including Muslim and Indigenous Tribal Peoples, wherever they may be found!

11

Mt. Sinai And
The Red Sea Crossing

One evening in the late spring of 1996, I had the privilege of personally meeting a part-time archaeologist named Ron Wyatt. He was on a speaking tour that brought him to a venue near to where I lived. Earlier that year, I had been reading with fascination, stories of how the Lord had guided Ron into making some astonishing archaeological discoveries. Now, I was to be a part of his audience.

He spoke with amazing authority, and yet presented himself humbly, captivating us all. During his discussion on the real Mt. Sinai and the Red Sea Crossing, you could hear a pin drop as everyone sat breathless while becoming instantly enmeshed in what was being shared. We were shown colour pictures that Ron had taken back in 1978 of two Phoenician style granite columns that were believed to be originally erected by King Solomon in commemoration of the Red Sea crossing by the Israelites. These pillars were originally positioned directly across the Gulf of Aqaba from each other, with one of the pillars being located on the Egyptian shoreline of Nuweba (an ancient flood plain) and the other, on an ancient Arabian (coastal) flood plain. The Red Sea (Gulf of Aqaba) spanned approximately eight miles wide between these two points.

Clinging to every word spoken by Ron, later that evening, I secretly asked the Lord for an opportunity to one day travel into the Sinai Peninsula and witness the crossing site and the pillar that was found on the beach in Nuweba for myself. I had no problem believing what had been shared that evening concerning the Red Sea Crossing, or the shocking fact that the true location of Mt. Sinai was actually in modern day Saudi Arabia. In biblical times, Saudi Arabia was known as the land of Midian. Holy Spirit gave me a strong witness to the truth of this matter, as it was being presented that evening.

The alleged true location of Mt. Sinai, believed by most throughout the ages of time as being correct, was actually assigned it's designation in the southern tip of the Sinai Peninsula by the unfounded traditions of Helena of Constantinople. As was common back in the day, many biblical sites were given specific designations without prior knowledge or substantiated evidence. Sadly, many of these biblical sites remain stuck in their traditional locations unchallenged; because of the fact it's good for tourism.

Every map that I am aware of, that can be found in our modern Bibles regarding the true location of Mt. Sinai is without question, incorrect! Holy Scripture actually reveals the correct location of Mt. Sinai. *But he who was of the bondwoman was born according to the flesh, and he of the freewoman through promise, which things are symbolic. For these are the two covenants: the one from Mount Sinai which gives birth to bondage, which is Hagar–for this Hagar is <u>Mount Sinai in Arabia</u>, and corresponds to Jerusalem which now is, and is in bondage with her children–but the Jerusalem above is free, which is the mother of us all.* Galatians 4:23-26.

I recommend to those of you who may be interested in researching further the things that have been shared thus far concerning the Red Sea Crossing, Mt. Sinai, and the Phoenician style granite columns, to search these things out on the internet. I also highly recommend that you Google; Jim & Penny Caldwell, Mountain of God, Interview 2009. You will be astounded!

12

Preparing For Nuweba

By divine providence, Monika and I found ourselves making travel arrangements to Israel so that we could attend the "Operation Exodus Ebenezer Emergency Fund–Twentieth Year Anniversary Celebration." The anniversary celebration was held in the city of Jerusalem, in January of 2011. While making our travel plans, I was reminded of the time back in 1996, when I asked the Lord for an opportunity to journey into the Sinai Peninsula for the purpose of visiting Nuweba, Solomon's Pillar and the staging ground of the actual Red Sea crossing point.

Inquiring of the Lord, Monika and I seemed to be getting a green light of approval to go ahead and make our Sinai trip arrangements before leaving for Israel.

While attending the conference, we met an American living in the Far East. This person was not known by us prior to that time. Over breakfast one morning, this person felt led to give us a parchment scroll that they had brought along from the Far East to give to a certain person or persons at the conference. Monika and I just happened to be those certain persons!

The parchment was a stunning watercolor painting of the Great Wall of China. Depicted in the background behind the Great Wall of China, was a beautiful portrayal of the ancient walls of Jerusalem. This painting was a prophetic depiction of the Silk Road Highway. The Silk Road Highway was a common trade route that connected the Far and Middle East together. Portions of this ancient highway are still intact to this day. The Silk Road Highway at one time was also used as an Aliyah Highway for the return of the exiled Jewish people back to Israel. Once again, this ancient highway is being used for that same purpose. God is calling forth and re-gathering from the four corners of the earth His covenant people the Jews, thus fulfilling what He decreed in times of old. I am certain that long before any of our travel plans into Egypt were ever made, the Lord had arranged for the parchment scroll to be given to us so that it could be brought along with us into the Sinai Peninsula. Something else of great importance was also to come along with us on this trip.

Before going further into the next part of this story, we need to re-visit what was shared earlier in chapter 10 regarding the significance of the prayer shirt that was given to us by the young Jewish man back in 1995.

Do you remember the prophetic covenant that was made between us, with the prayer shirt being the symbolic seal of that covenant? Do you remember that he further believed that together Jew and Gentile would find salvation in the living Messiah of the Bible? Do you also remember how he spoke prophetically over us, believing that we would be able to reach the Jewish people with a message of God's unfailing love in a very special way–travelling into certain places that he would be unable to go to himself? We certainly remembered that eventful day.

Since that incredible day, we have kept in our possession the young Jewish man's prayer shirt. His precious gift enabled us on numerous occasions to use the prayer shirt as a catalyst for prophetic ministry. For example, not only did the prayer shirt make its way to the Ukraine in 1997 with us, it eventually made its way back to Jerusalem and the Sinai Peninsula in 2011!

Immediately   following   the   "Ebenezer   twentieth

Anni-versary/Ministry Conference," Monika and I had the rare opportunity of getting up onto the Temple Mount in Jerusalem with the pray shirt and our flag of Israel. Our intentions were to bring the prayer shirt right to the Golden Gate, also known as the Eastern Gate. From that strategic point, we were able to intercede through prayer, items of concern regarding the Jewish People. Through the symbolism of the prayer shirt, we petitioned the Lord, reminding Him of His covenantal promises concerning the re-gathering of His ancient people from the four corners of the world. Un-noticed by anyone, we continued with our prayers, asking the Lord to re-open the spiritual Aliyah highways, starting with the opening of the spiritual Golden Gate!

While under the anointing of Holy Spirit–we made our way to the Dome of The Spirits located on the north side of the Dome of The Rock. When it was safe to do so, I held up the prayer shirt directly under the Dome of The Spirits, and prayed further into God's plan for global Aliyah with Monika. We also offered up intercessory prayers on behalf of the young Jewish man and his family.

13

The Adventure Begins

On January 27th, 2011, after leaving behind our bulky luggage in a secure location in Jerusalem, we began our journey to Nuweba. Arrangements to be personally picked up from the Taba Border Crossing were made in advance with the owner of the hotel that we would be staying at. We traveled by bus from the Central Bus Station in Jerusalem to the city of Eilat. While on the bus to Eilat, I had many questions that needed answering. For example, how were we to get to the Taba crossing? At what time of day would we cross the border? Would we actually meet our Egyptian shuttle driver from the resort? How long could we stay? Would we actually find Solomon's Pillar, or the beach that the ancient Israelites crossed over from, and would we encounter any unrest or violence?

On the day of our crossing the border into Egypt, all Hell was breaking loose in Cairo! Protests, up-risings and violence were rampant throughout the city. All of this was happening while walking across the Taba Border on foot. Going through customs was a bureaucratic nightmare, to say the very least, but praise the Lord, we made it with the prayer shirt, flag of Israel, Canadian flag, and parchment scroll!

Much to our relief, our driver arrived approximately a half hour later. So far everything was going as God had planned.

As we wound our way along the rugged Aqaba coast, the stark contrast of the pristine aqua-marine blue waters of the Red Sea, and the hostile dessert environment, had a beauty almost beyond description. Looking out over the waters, we could see the coastal mountain range of Saudi Arabia. Somewhere in those mountains stood Mt. Sinai!

We were living our dream. Soon we would be at our destination. Only the Lord knew what glorious treasures awaited us. One of the most unusual observations that Monika and I noticed while on our way, was the fact that every little village that we passed seemed to be completely void of any inhabitants. Resort after resort was empty. Nobody seemed to be around. We were the only vehicle on the entire coastal highway. I was beginning to be a little concerned, but knowing that we were living out our destiny, those feelings were quickly erased when we pulled up in front of our lavish new resort home.

Two hotel servants greeted us. They would not allow Monika or me to handle what little luggage we had. For the duration of our visit, they became our personal servants and quickly became our newest friends. The resort owner had been waiting for our safe arrival and immediately welcomed us as if we were his own family. We had such favor, with more to come. We were brought to our grand palace of a room. The view from our balcony was amazing. From our vantage point, we could see the beach and the Red Sea, framed by swaying palms. Contrasted behind this fabulous scene were the coastal mountains of Arabia right across the eight mile stretch of the Gulf. Looking around our well appointed room, we offered up prayers of thanksgiving to God for His faithfulness.

After resting awhile, we had an opportunity to meet up with the hotel owner by the pool. He was completely intrigued by our visit to his resort. He could not figure out why two Canadians would come all this way for just a few days rest and relaxation. We excitedly began to share with him the reasons for our brief visit. His mouth dropped wide open. He asked if we knew of anyone else's soon arrival to his resort. Looking around, for the first time, we realized that we were the only guests registered in the entire resort, except for one older couple from England. Answering his question, we said that we knew of no one. He went on to explain that part of a professional dive team working with a film production company would be checking in later on in the afternoon. He also shared with us that they were hoping to film some underwater footage that would become part of a film documentary regarding the Red Sea crossing. We found out later that this film was seven years in the making and would be titled; Exodus Conspiracy. The rest of the afternoon evaporated away over endless talk about the second exodus! The hotel owner insisted that Monika and I have dinner with these very special guests. He made all of the arrangements and appropriate introductions.

Just before dinner, there was another opportunity for Monika and I to meet up with the hotel owner. We shared with him our concern about how we would get to the location of Solomon's Pillar and the actual beach head where the pillar was first discovered. Without hesitation he offered to take us personally to both sites in his jeep! He also offered to take us up into the actual wadi that the ancient Israelites traveled through from the land of Goshen. This ancient highway was actually the only trade route carved through the impassable dessert mountains by nature itself. Now it is a paved highway connecting the Sinai Peninsula to the rest of Egypt. Once again, we felt God's favor over the importance of this special prayer journey of discovery.

I was more than thrilled to meet our new hotel guests over dinner. We compared notes, talking late into the night about Ron Wyatt's discoveries and those of Jim and Penny Caldwell. We spoke of the natural underwater land bridge that connected the two beach heads. The Gulf of Aqaba is over five thousand feet deep, and yet at the actual crossing point, precisely where the waters once parted, can be found the natural underwater land bridge. The land bridge is approximately four or five kilometers wide reaching all the way across the gulf to the ancient land of Midian on the not too distant shore. The ocean depth at the land bridge is only a few hundred feet, with an almost perfect three to four degree slope, making for easy travel. Only the Lord could arrange such geographical wonders or such meetings!

14

The Beach Head
And Solomon's Pillar

Early the next morning Monika and I watched in complete wonder one of the most beautiful sunrises that we have ever seen. The golden-orange sun was rising over the Arabian mountains. Somewhere out there was the true Mt. Sinai, but for the moment we were just enjoying the incredible experience of being in a foreign land so far from home.

We were served a four course royal breakfast complete with personalized service. Our servants stood alongside our dining table ensuring that our slightest desires were met. Monika and I were strangers to this unique culture of hospitality and faithful dedication.

After breakfast the film crew prepared themselves for a day of underwater exploration and filming, while we prepared ourselves to join up with our host who became our personal guide. We were pumped for a day of serious exploration! After spending just a little time with our new found friend we were amazed as to how much he actually knew regarding the history of the exodus of the Jews from Egypt and about the true location of Mt. Sinai.

It was a short ten minute ride to the Nuweba beach staging ground. I was trembling with pure excitement as I climbed out of the jeep. This vast area could easily accommodate a huge multitude of people. We were shown where the pillar was first discovered, and told of its present location. Many pictures of this historic beach were taken.

While standing on the beach, our guide pointed out something very unusual. The beach looked like a sheet of broken glass. On closer inspection we could see that all of the small pebbles and rocks were actually melted into the sand in such a way that the sand and pebbles were like a huge shinny glass surface. This strange anomaly could be observed for a few kilometers down the beach. Our guide explained that he believed that the high heat source needed to create such a condition could possibly have been generated from the pillar of fire that protected the Israelites from the advances of Pharaoh's army.

Our next stop would be Solomon's pillar! Within five minutes we were there. What a sight to behold. It was true, the pillar actually existed. Without delay, I stood beside the column with the prayer shirt, parchment scroll, and flags of Israel and Canada. Our host became very nervous when the flag of Israel was displayed. He didn't feel like getting put in jail or worse! Monika took some very quick pictures. We then prayed like we did on the Temple Mount.

Our guide had many more interesting things to share with us regarding this area. Another major highlight for us was the experience of our next destination. We were able to drive into the wadi that the Israelites would have travelled through. Many pictures were taken of the steep boxed canyon walls and surrounding topography. About one hour into the snaking canyon, we found a perfect spot to take in the sights and lay down on the dessert floor our Israel and Canadian flags. Our guide was not nearly as nervous this time. Maybe he was getting a little more used to our way of doing things. More declarations and prayers were offered up.

It was late afternoon when we arrived back at the resort. Our guide offered to take us snorkel diving out on the coral reefs. How could we refuse? He was a professional scuba diver and knew every square inch of those reefs. The Gulf of Aqaba has some of the best diving conditions in the world.

The marine life, coral and unlimited visibility is absolutely outrageous. We could stay out for hours because of the warm bath-like temperatures. Our guide took underwater pictures of our experience. He also pointed out to us the gentle slope of the ocean floor. We could actually see this amazing phenomenon as far as ocean visibility would allow.

The next day was time to say good bye. We needed to get back to Israel before conditions worsened in Cairo. Early in the morning Monika and I finished up our prayer journey by going down to the water's edge. Placing the prayer shirt over my shoulders, while draping the flag of Israel over one arm and the flag of Canada over the other, and while holding the parchment scroll over my head, intercessory prayers were offered up to the Lord regarding global Aliyah. Monika repeated the same procedures.

Reminding the Lord about how He once parted the physical Red Sea, we asked if He would once again part the spiritual waters of the Red Sea symbolizing the opening of the Aliyah highways.

There were just two things left that needed to be done. The first thing was the importance of dipping the prayer shirt into the Red Sea at the crossing point, and the second thing, the dipping of my Star of David necklace that was given to me by my father into the Red Sea. All was done. Mission accomplished!

Scripture References Concerning The Re-Gathering Of The Jewish People
(Taken from the NLT)

But forget all that–it is nothing compared to what I am going to do. For I am about to do a brand-new thing. See, I have already begun! Do you not see it? I will make a pathway through the wilderness for My people to come home. I will create rivers for them in the desert! Isaiah 43:18, 19.

But the time is coming, says the Lord, when people who are taking an oath will no longer say, as surely as the Lord lives, who rescued the people of Israel from the land of Egypt. Instead, they will say, as surely as the Lord lives, who brought the people of Israel back to their own land from the land of the north and from all the countries to which He had exiled them. For I will bring them back to this land that I gave their ancestors. Jeremiah 16:14, 15.

In that day, says the Lord, when people are taking an oath, they will no longer say, as surely as the Lord lives, who rescued the people of Israel from the land of Egypt. Instead, they will say, as surely as the Lord lives, who brought the people of Israel back to their own land from the land of the north and from all the countries to which He had exiled them. Then they will live in their own land. Jeremiah 23: 7, 8.

I will bring them back home to their own land of Israel from among the peoples and nations. I will feed them on the mountains of Israel and by the rivers in all the places where people live. Ezekiel 34:13.

Do not be afraid, for I am with you. I will gather you and your children from east and west and from north and south. I will bring My sons and daughters back to Israel from the distant corners of the earth. Isaiah 43:5, 6.

For I will bring them from the north and from the distant corners of the earth. I will not forget the blind and lame, the expectant mothers and women about to give birth. A great company will return! Jeremiah 31:8.

I will bring my exiled people of Israel back from distant lands, and they will rebuild their ruined cities and live in them again. They will plant vineyards and gardens; they will eat their crops and drink their wine. I will firmly plant them there in the land I have given them, says the Lord your God. Then they will never be uprooted again. Amos 9:14, 15.

Section "B"

15

True Faith, Wealth & Prosperity

I realize that what I have shared with you thus far concerning my life story was fairly lengthy and detailed. I hope that in the sharing of these details, you will better understand who I am as a person today. Insights given to me from the Lord through the shaping of my character are the things I wish to now spring board from. God has an amazing eternal plan for us based on the mysteries of Christ that are hidden in the development of our character. I invite you to come along with me a little further, and explore the true nature of God's heart concerning the things that really matter.

The level of faith that can be developed by making wise choices through our personal circumstances in this physical earth realm will become the bases in part for the realms of responsibility that will be given to us to operate in during the ages to come.God our heavenly Father is pleased when the outer limits of our faith potential can be challenged by Godly coaxing by Holy Spirit. This type of faith is not to develop worldly monetary prosperity or wealth, this type of activity has the potential of being very deceptive. True faith, wealth and prosperity on the other hand, are developed in the school of suffering while being in the furnace of affliction. The trials of life enables or gives us the opportunity to learn the art of overcoming through our personal circumstances so that we can begin to experience victorious living from out of what we have learned.

The dreams of break-through, reconciliation, restoration and victorious prosperous living that we desire for ourselves, our families/extended families, neighbors, co-workers or even complete strangers that may enter within our gates can become an awesome reality when we put into practice the very faith that we are developing by the coaxing of Holy Spirit. True wealth and prosperity is when our soul prospers. Our heavenly Father loves this type of prosperity when it operates in our personal lives.

There has been much teaching by certain individuals concerning the angel of finance. Apparently at least one of these individuals has claimed to have been taken up in the spirit by the angel of finance into the treasure rooms of Heaven. He was shown treasure troves of riches that were there for the taking. This individual recounted how he stuffed his pockets, his shirt, and his jacket full of gold coins and other treasures from vast gold chests. I have often wondered if this undertaking is scriptural.

The Bible does speak of an angel of finance. Let's have a look at Luke 4:5-8. *Then the Devil took Him up and revealed to Him all the kingdoms of the world in a moment of time. The Devil told Him, "I will give You the glory* (the riches, honors, and grandeur belonging to them) *of these kingdoms and authority over them – because they are mine to give to anyone I please. I will give it all to You if You will bow down and worship me." Jesus replied, "The Scriptures say, 'You must worship the Lord your God; serve only Him."* NLT.

In 2 Corinthians 11:14 we are told that Satan can appear as an angel of light; *...But I am not surprised! Even Satan can disguise himself as an angel of light.* NLT. If Satan can disguise himself as an angel of light, then he certainly can make a claim that he is also the angel of finance. Nowhere in Scripture have I been able to find that God has taken back the kingdoms of this world and their riches in the context of this present age. So at least for the moment, it seems to me that Satan still has control over the wealth of this world (Babylon). Take heed! There is much deception being taught in the Church today concerning kingdom finances, riches and wealth by supposed anointed men of God.

True and everlasting prosperity can only be found in our eternal inheritance. Worldly prosperity in this physical realm is not lasting and only temporary in nature. I believe that by God given faith, it is possible and desirable for Spirit led persons to tap into their own heavenly inheritance and from that, begin reaching out to the multitudes of humanity, especially to the poor and needy, the orphans, widows, and the lonely elderly. To receive the true riches of Heaven, we must be weaned from the carnal wealth of this world. What a wonderful opportunity we have in helping others build their spiritual kingdoms in Christ, by tapping into our own inheritance and then giving out to others from our inheritance. In saying this, I am reminded of what Jesus said; *"With God all things are possible."* I believe that the Lord has given us this revelation based on I Timothy 6:17-19. *Command those who are rich in this present age not to be haughty, nor to trust in uncertain riches but in the living God, who gives us richly all things to enjoy. Let them do good, that they be rich in good works, ready to give, willing to share, storing up for themselves a good foundation for the time to come, that they may lay hold on eternal life.*

There seems to be a fair amount of emphasis on a passage of Scripture found in Proverbs 13:22 that speak of the world's wealth or the wealth of the sinner being stored up for the righteous. I believe that the transference of the wealth spoken of in Proverbs 13:22 is referring to the particular history of that specific time. Based upon this passage, somehow we are led to believe that a great transference of wealth is about to take place in the believers life that will enhance his/her ability to usher in God's kingdom. This belief most certainly may be true only in part. Let us now have a look at that verse; *A good man leaves an inheritance to his children's children, but the wealth of the sinner is stored up for the righteous.*

I believe that one of the keys to understanding the above mentioned passage for our present age can be found in a parable that is taught by Jesus Christ in Luke 19:12-27;

Therefore He said: "A certain nobleman went into a far country to receive for himself a kingdom and to return. So he called ten of his servants, delivered to them ten minas, and said to them, "Do business till I come." But his citizens hated him, and sent a delegation after him, saying, "We will not have this man to reign over us." And so it was that when he returned, having received the kingdom, he then commanded these servants, to whom he had given the money, to be called to him, that he might know how much every man had gained by trading. Then came the first, saying, "Master, your mina has earned ten minas." And he said to him, "Well done, good servant; because you were faithful in a very little, have authority over ten cities." And the second came, saying, "Master, your mina has earned five minas." Likewise he said to him, "You also be over five cities." Then another came, saying, "Master, here is your mina, which I have kept put away in a handkerchief. For I feared you, because you are an austere man. You collect what you did not deposit, and reap what you did not sow." And he said to him, "Out of your own mouth I will judge you, you wicked servant. You knew that I was an austere man, collecting what I did not deposit and reaping what I did not sow. Why then did you not put my money in the bank, that at my coming I might have collected it with interest?" And he said to those who stood by, "Take the mina from him, and give it to him who has ten minas" (But they said to him, "Master, he has ten minas.") "For I say to you, that to everyone who has will be given; and from him who does not have, even what he has will be taken away from him. But bring here those enemies of mine, who did not want me to reign over them, and slay them before me."

The mina that was given to each of the ten servants in this parable represents their inheritance (true wealth), and not worldly monetary wealth. When we go out into all of the world to share the good news of Jesus the Christ and His kingdom, we have the opportunity to share this good news from the very substance of our own inheritance.

Some will do well with the good news as they receive it, and will begin to have their Godly kingdoms in Christ be built, while others will lose the potential of their inheritance and the building of their kingdoms without Christ, because of unbelief (no faith). In fact, the parable just read says; *"For I say to you, that to everyone who has will be given; and from him who does not have, even what he has will be taken away from him."*

Perhaps the wealth of the sinner that is being stored up for the righteous is indeed the potential of their (the sinner's) inheritance. I believe that our true inheritance is all of God's promises that He has for us. Godly wisdom, the revelation of hidden mysteries in God's ever unfolding creation, the amazing works of Christ that manifest in and through our lives, partaking in God's glory, ruling and reigning with His Son Jesus the Christ and much more are the things of our inheritance. Monetary wealth and prosperity as defined in Christendom can take second place as far as I am concerned. Perhaps when we now read what Jesus has to say in Matthew 19:23-30, we will have a new perspective on true wealth and prosperity.

Then Jesus said to His disciples, "Assuredly, I say to you that it is hard for a rich man to enter the kingdom of Heaven. And again I say to you, it is easier for a camel to go through the eye of a needle than for a rich man to enter the kingdom of God." When His disciples heard it, they were greatly astonished saying, "Who then can be saved?" But Jesus looked at them and said to them, "With men this is impossible, but with God all things are possible." Then Peter answered and said to Him, "See, we have left all and followed You. Therefore what shall we have?" So Jesus said to them, "Assuredly I say to you, that in the regeneration, when the Son of Man sits on the throne of His glory, you who have followed Me will also sit on twelve thrones, judging the twelve tribes of Israel. And everyone who has left houses or brothers or sisters or father or mother or wife or children or lands, for My name's sake, shall receive a hundredfold, and inherit eternal life. But many who are first will be last, and the last first."

And He said to them, "Take heed and beware of covetousness, for one's life does not consist in the abundance of the things he possesses." Luke 12:15.

But seek the kingdom of God, and all these things shall be added to you. "Do not fear, little flock, for it is your Father's good pleasure to give you the kingdom. Sell what you have and give alms; provide yourselves money bags which do not grow old, a treasure in the heavens that does not fail, where no thief approaches nor moth destroys. Luke 12: 31-33.

Now godliness with contentment is great gain. For we brought nothing into this world, and it is certain we can carry nothing out. And having food and clothing, with these we shall be content. But those who desire to be rich fall into temptation and a snare, and into many foolish and harmful lusts which drown men in destruction and perdition. For the love of money is a root of all kinds of evil, for which some have strayed from the faith in their greediness, and pierced themselves through with many sorrows. But you, O man of God, flee these things and pursue righteousness, godliness, faith, love, patience, gentleness. 1 Timothy 6:6-11.

Listen, my beloved brethren: Has God not chosen the poor of this world to be rich in faith and heirs of the kingdom which He promised to those who love Him? James 2:5.

In conclusion to what has been shared thus far on the topic of true faith, wealth and prosperity, yet another amazing passage of Scripture can be found in the book of Acts 3:1-8.

Now Peter and John went up together to the temple at the hour of prayer, the ninth hour. And a certain man lame from his mother's womb was carried, whom they laid daily at the gate of the temple which is called Beautiful, to ask alms from those who entered the temple; who, seeing Peter and John about to go into the temple, asked for alms. And fixing his eyes on him, with John, Peter said, "Look at us." So he gave them his attention, expecting to receive something from them. Then Peter said, "Silver and gold I do not have, but what I do have I give you: In the name of Jesus Christ of Nazareth, rise up and walk." And he took him by the right hand and lifted him up, and immediately his feet and ankle bones received strength. So he, leaping up, stood and walked and entered the temple with them - walking, leaping, and praising God.

The Apostle Peter was operating in the realm of anointing that came from him tapping into his inheritance. The anointing empowered the spoken word of healing that the Apostle Peter commanded over the lame man. His body, soul and spirit had no choice but to simply respond to the authority of the command, thus his healing came. Notice that before the Apostle Peter spoke the command of healing for release of the blessing, he made it known to the many witnesses standing by that he was not operating from out of the world's physical realm of prosperity or wealth.

The Apostle Peter declared; *"Silver and gold I do not have, but what I do have I give you: In the name of Jesus Christ of Nazareth, rise up and walk."* It was the anointing that came from his inheritance that commanded the blessing. This is where true faith, wealth and prosperity are to be found. Jesus is speaking to us about personal sacrifice as we give from out of ourselves, helping better the lives of others. In so doing, I believe we will receive a tremendous blessing in return. To God be given all the glory, amen!

16

The Trials
And Tribulations Of Life

Please consider with me James 1:2; *Dear brothers and sisters, whenever trouble comes your way, let it be an opportunity for joy.*

1 Peter 1:6, 7; *So be truly glad! There is wonderful joy ahead, even though it is necessary for you to endure many trials for a while.These trials are only to test your faith, to show that it is strong and pure. It is being tested as fire tests and purifies gold – and your faith is far more precious to God than mere gold. So if your faith remains strong after being tried by fiery trials, it will bring you much praise and glory and honor on the day when Jesus Christ is revealed to the whole world.*

John 16:33; *I have told you all this so that you may have peace in Me. Here on earth you will have many trials and sorrows. But take heart, because I have overcome the world.*

Acts 20:19; *I have done the Lord's work humbly – yes, and with tears. I have endured the trials that came to me from the plots of the Jews.*

Romans 5:3; *We can rejoice, too, when we run into problems and trials, for we know that they are good for us – they help us learn to endure.*1 Peter 4:12,13; *Dear friends, don't be surprised at the fiery trials you are going through, as if* *something strange were happening to you.Instead, be very glad – because these trials will make you partners with Christ in His suffering, and afterward you will have the wonderful joy of sharing His glory when it is displayed to all the world.*

Matthew 24:9; *Then you will be arrested, persecuted, and killed. You will be hated all over the world because of your allegiance to Me.*Romans 12:12; *Be glad for all God is planning for you. Be patient in trouble, and always be prayerful.* Romans 8:35; *Can anything ever separate us from Christ's love? Does it mean He no longer loves us if we have trouble or calamity, or are persecuted, or are hungry or cold or in danger or threatened with death?*

Revelation 1:9; *I am John, your brother. In Jesus we are partners in suffering and in the Kingdom and in patient endurance. I was exiled to the island of Patmos for preaching the word of God and speaking about Jesus.*

Revelation 2:10; *Don't be afraid of what you are about to suffer. The Devil will throw some of you into prison and put you to the test. You will be persecuted for ten days. Remain faithful even when facing death, and I will give you the crown of life.*

1 Thessalonians 1:6; *So you received the message with joy from the Holy Spirit in spite of the severe suffering it brought you. In this way, you imitated both us and the Lord.* (All of the above mentioned Scripture passages were taken from the NLT).

All of God's testing's of humanity throughout the history of the world are absolutely necessary for the perfecting of the saints. His eternal plans for each of us are filled with purpose. Amazingly this does not ever interfere with the working out of our salvation with fear and trembling. Each of our life experiences has significance and carries eternal weight. God is very interested in the condition of our hearts, and attitudes towards Him. This interest is not so much for His benefit, but rather, more for ours. He desires that we discover where we are at in our character development, thus His interest.

God will ultimately turn all of our experiences for good,

and especially to those who love Him. The level of faith (belief) that we develop through our personal circumstances by the choices we make in this life, will become the bases in part for what realm of responsibility we will be given to operate in during the ages to come. Desirable faith is not faith to develop worldly monetary prosperity or wealth. True wealth is when our soul prospers. Our heavenly Father loves this type of prosperity operating in our personal lives very much. Faith that is developed in the school of suffering while being in the furnace of affliction (the trials of life) enables or gives us the opportunity to learn the art of overcoming through our circumstances so that we can begin to experience victorious living from out of what we have learned. Dreams of break-through, and victorious prosperous living that we may have for ourselves, our families/extended families, neighbors, co-workers or even complete strangers that may enter within our gates can become an awesome reality if we put into practice the very faith that is developing by the coaxing of Holy Spirit.

17

Gold, Silver, Precious Stones

On one side of the spiritual coin, we have been exposed and overly saturated with terminologies and manifestations such as signs and wonders, miracles, prosperity and health, success, anointing, healings, open heavens, the fire of God, revival and the great harvest, soaking in the Spirit, prophetic declarations, the promises of God, the raising of the dead and many more terms, conditions, and manifestations coming at us at lightning speed. It boggles the mind to even try and keep up with it all!

Even with all of this (questionable?) activity, it is possible to find Truth and relevance in the things just mentioned. However, I believe that a much deeper revelation of truth and understanding can only come about when we meet God in the furnace of affliction. Please note: When referring to; *"terminologies and manifestations such as signs and wonders, miracles, prosperity and health, success, anointing, healing, open heavens, the fire of God, revival and the great harvest, soaking in the Spirit, prophetic declarations, the promises of God, the raising of the dead and many more terms, conditions, and manifestations that are coming at us at lightning speed"* as questionable, I do believe with all of my heart in the legitimacy of all of the above mentioned manifestations provided they are authentic! Sadly, particularly here in the western hemisphere, often times there is a blatant abuse of these gifts with much counterfeiting of the authentic gifts of Holy Spirit being administered by so called men and women of God. For a price, we can purchase our healings, blessings, and prophetic words and God only knows what else–for a first-fruits, or seed offering. In our quest for the anointing etc. we tend to make super stars out of earthen vessels (Christian leaders). How far must we fall before being morally bankrupt?

The whole point of what I am trying to say is this. We put so much emphasis on the prosperity side of the spiritual coin, when in fact we desperately need to be counter-balanced with a precise measure of suffering and sorrow by the hand of God to help in the forging of our character. Please do not misunderstand what I am trying to say here. Truth can be found in these movements; however, error has a way of being mixed in with truth by Satan's design. We must practice diligence by constantly looking for good and lasting fruit regardless of the movement.

On the other side of the spiritual coin is something far greater that needs to come to light. We desperately need this aspect of God's truth, because I believe it is the most important key to understanding our destiny. The gold, silver, precious stones, and the crowns all tie into why we are to be over comers in this life.

While it is yet day regardless of our personal circumstances, we have been given the opportunity to fight the good fight of faith, and to run the race, so that we may receive a prize. The rewards that are to be given will be everlasting and will never fade. The Bible teaches that we will be rewarded for any worthy works, and that Christ will discriminate them from those that will be burned at the judgment seat. Works which result from our living union with Christ through Holy Spirit will be rewarded! The works that will be rewarded are easy to recognize. They bear his likeness and they are works God purposed from the very beginning as a result that would come from out of our relationship to Him.

Three kinds of works;
  1) Gold
  2) Silver
  3) Precious Stones

  1) Gold: That which has been tried and approved through waiting in faith. We are said to buy gold when we come to know God through experience in trials of faith and patience. God speaks of the character we develop through meeting God in the furnace of affliction. Revelation 3:8; Job 23:10; 1 Peter1:7; James 1:2-4; Proverbs 17:3.
  2) Silver: The purification of motive and character that results from God's refining. As the promise God has given us is put to the test, our character is developed in trust, dependence upon God, and purity of motive. The dross of selfishness is removed. Malachi 3:3; Zechariah 13:9; Psalms 66:10.
  3) Precious Stones: The values that are established within us through the choices made under pressure. Our character is formed as we encounter afflictions in which the grace of God comes to us to respond to them on the basis of his priorities. Precious stones are those things we hold most dear. Our heart is where our treasure is. Jeremiah 15:19; Revelation 21:19-21; Isaiah 54:11-14; Malachi 3:16-18.

In contrast, the works to be burned are those that did not become "fire proof" during this life. They are the products of self-effort instead of dependency on His indwelling Spirit of life. Because they are not the fruit of our union with Christ, they are devoid of His life and are considered "dead works."
Three kinds of dead works;
  1) Hay
  2) Wood
  3) Stubble

1) Hay: Things we do to impress others by means of appearance, personality, or status. We can make people think we are more than we are, but God sees the heart. Popularity is short-lived. Reality soon catches up with us, and our outward appeal soon withers. 1 Peter 1:24; Psalms 103:15, 16; Isaiah 40:6-8; James 1:10, 11.

2) Wood: The works of our own hands, or the result of our natural talent unaided by Holy Spirit. Those who are talented are often tempted to idolize their own creativity, ingenuity, and skill. These things are good, but they are not of lasting value. They can become occasions for idolatry. Deuteronomy 4:28; Daniel 5:4, 23; Daniel 15:4; 2 Kings 19:18; Romans 1:25.

3) Stubble: The non-essentials in our lives that should be pruned away to make for greater fruitfulness. In the natural, stubble is the short standing straw left behind after reaping. At harvest time it is burned. Job 21:18; Isaiah 5:21-24; Isaiah 33:11, 12; Obadiah: 17, 18; Malachi 4:1; John 15:1-6.

18

The Five Crowns & Rewards

Some believers will receive greater rewards than others, some will suffer loss. If a man's work abides which he hath built there upon, he shall receive a reward. *If any man's work shall be burned, he shall suffer loss, but he himself shall be saved; yet so as by fire.* 1 Corinthians 3:14, 15. Malachi 3:2, 3.

Rewards are described in the Bible as crowns. Crowns speak of public recognition and honor. As believers, we are often devalued, misunderstood, unrewarded, and even persecuted. But on that day we shall all receive due recognition for all we have done and become for Christ's sake. The praise of men will look so dim in the light of his glorious recognition. These crowns will demonstrate Christ's approval of us and His acceptance of our work. 2 Corinthians 5:9. There are five crowns mentioned in Scripture, each given for a specific accomplishment.

1) Crown of Life for faithfulness. James 1:12; Revelation 2:10.
2) Crown of Glory for the under-shepherd. 1 Peter 5:1-4
3) Crown of Righteousness for loving His appearing. 2 Timothy 4:7, 8.
4) Crown of Rejoicing for soul-winning. 1 Thessalonians 2:19.

5) The Incorruptible Crown for self-mastery. 1 Corinthians 9: 25.

These crowns are set before us in Scripture to motivate us in this life. God wants us to thoroughly invest ourselves in competing for the prize. 1 Corinthians 9:24, 25; 2 John: 8. Scripture warns us to strive for mastery with strong determination not to lose our reward. Winning the race requires whole hearted application in zeal and self-discipline.

19

Works To Be Judged

A) Stewardship: Care and use of all God has committed to us.
   1) Time: Ephesians 5:16; Colossians 4:5; 1 Peter 1:17; Psalms 90:12.
   2) Money: 2 Corinthians 9:6, 7; 1 Corinthians 16:2.
   3) Opportunities to share Christ. Proverbs 11:30; Daniel 12:3; 1 Thessalonians 2:19, 20.
   4) God's gifts and graces. Luke 19:11-26; 2 Timothy 1:6; 1 Corinthians 12:4-11.
B) Relationships: How we treat other believers and discern the body of Christ. Matthew 10:41,42; Hebrews 6:10; Romans 14:10-12; 1 Corinthians 11:29; Galatians 3:28.
C) Our reaction to suffering for Christ. Matthew 5:11, 12; 1 Peter 2:19, 20; 1Peter 4:12-19.
D) Our personal discipline–or how we run the race. 1 Corinthians 9:24-27; Philippians 3:13, 14.
E) Our overcoming of temptation. James 1:2, 3; Revelation 12:11.
F) Personal fruitfulness–Character development into the likeness of Christ. Galatians 5:22, 23; 2 Peter 1:2-12; Mark 11:12-14; John 15:1-11.
G) Our exercise of authority over others. Hebrews 13:17; James 3: 1; Acts 20:26-28.

The crowns, gold, silver, and precious stones come under the principles of how the universe is being operated. The ultimate goal of the universe is for the Bride of Christ. Romans 8:28; Ephesians 3: 9–11. Scripture reveals what God has done from eternity past and all that He will do until the "Marriage Supper of The Lamb." He is gathering out and training His Bride for her exalted position of co-rulership with His Son over His vast, ever expanding, eternal Kingdom in the ages to come. Only after the Bride is on the throne with Jesus Christ, will God be ready to unveil His creative program for the eternal ages to come.

Suffering in the furnace of affliction is in addition to overcoming through the power of prayer. If we overcome, we shall reign. Revelation 3:21. If we suffer, we shall also reign. 2 Timothy 2:12.

God designed the system of prayer to equip or qualify the Bride of Christ with the techniques, skills, and the know-how for rulership. By God's design, suffering, which is the consequence of the fall, will produce our character, disposition, and compassionate spirit, which will be required for rulers in a government where the law of love is supreme.

All those who are born again of the spirit (sons and daughters of God) are in training to be rulers. Since the supreme law of the future social order, called the kingdom of God, is for the learning of deep dimensions of this love, this love can only be learned in the school of suffering.[3] Even after the new birth and the in filling of Holy Spirit, the elements of our salvation are developed by exercise and testing. Purity is one thing and maturity is another. Maturity comes through times of suffering. If we suffer, we shall also reign, because where there is little suffering there is little love, no suffering no love–no love, no ruling. When we are born again, we immediately enter into apprenticeship for ruling. Since agape love is an essential qualification for the exercise of authority in the heavenly social order, this apprenticeship is for the development of this love. Agape love is the love which loves because of its own inherent nature, not because of the excellence or worth of its object. It is spontaneous, automatic love.

Tribulation is necessary for the decentralization of self.

Because self prohibits the development of deep dimensions of agape love, this love can be developed only in the school of suffering. It grows and develops by exercise and testing. This may explain the relationship between sainthood and suffering, by showing why there is no sainthood without suffering. It may also show why the greatest saints are often the greatest sufferers.

No one ever becomes a saint without suffering because suffering when properly accepted is the pathway to glory. Because this is true, learning agape love by the example of Christ is the supreme purpose of life on earth. Our Father's primary occupation in this age is not regulating the universe by the mighty power of His command, but it is teaching the Bride-of-Christ-elect the lessons of agape love in preparation for the throne. Our Father does nothing in the realm of redemption that is not related to the task. Every single incident, whether joy, sorrow, pain, pleasure, or blessing without exception is being utilized by our Father for the purpose of maturing us in agape love. Thus, the supreme purpose of life on earth is not pleasure, fame, wealth, or any other form of worldly success, but learning agape love.

Eternal rank will be determined not by talent, magnetic personality, intellect, earthly success and affluence, but by one thing and one thing only–agape love. Please read Mathew 20:25-28. There is no love without self giving. No self giving without pain. No love without suffering.

Suffering is an essential ingredient of agape love. Our Father cannot love without cost. Think what it cost our Father to give His Son to die as a sin offering on the cross. What did it cost our Father to turn His face away from His innocent Son and forsake Him who did not sin but whom, for our sakes, became sin? 2 Corinthians 5:21. Think what it must have cost God to pour out upon His Son on the cross, the full fury of His own wrath against sin, because of the guilt of all the sin of mankind. Hebrews 2:9.

The Apostle Paul said; *"Love suffers."* 1 Corinthians 13:4. This means that love must suffer voluntarily. God is love, but there is no love without voluntary suffering. Love that does not accept suffering voluntarily is a misnomer, for the essence of love is the decentralization of self. Decentralization without voluntary acceptance of suffering cannot happen.

Absolute truth is this; there is no character development without suffering. Suffering is the cornerstone of the universe because, without it there is no decentralization of self and therefore no agape love. There is no such thing as a saint who has not suffered.

Because Christ could not make a full atonement for sin without absorbing its full consequences in His own person and being, no human being can ever suffer a pain, sorrow, heart ache, or disappointment that Christ has not already experienced in His own person. This means that every person is legally delivered from the full penalty, all the bitter fruits of sin and the fall. This penalty cannot legally be collected the second time. Isaiah 53 says; *"By His stripes we are healed."* If so, then every person is legally delivered from all sickness, disease, pain, sorrow, poverty and limitations of every kind.

Please note: What I believe Scripture is meaning to say; *"by His strips we are healed"* is this. The Bible tells us that the wages of sin is death. By the strips of Jesus, we were rescued from eternal death! He paid that price on our behalf. The healing that humanity will ultimately receive by the strips of Jesus is Life from the dead. This may include health, wealth, and healing, but more than likely it is a prospering soul that the strips of Jesus paid for. A prospering soul has profound eternal significance. This is where true victory can be found. Much warfare is fought in the mind and because of that, we are commanded to have the mind of Christ. Victory over disease and poverty in the physical realm is included in the strips of Jesus; however a prospering soul comes about by overcoming.

We can only activate the reality of this truth by becoming a believer of this truth through the finished work of Jesus Christ. Those, whom choose not to believe, will walk all of their earthly days in total defeat of this understanding. God's mercy will ultimately triumph over our defeats through His judgments, but why wait for such a time, when we can come to Him right now while it is yet day!

Let us have a look at an amazing Scripture verse that says; *It is a trustworthy statement deserving full acceptance. For it is for this we labor and strive, because we have fixed our hope on the living God, who is the Savior of all men, especially of believers. Prescribe and teach these things.* 1 Timothy 4:9-11. Notice the words, *"Savior of all men especially of believers."* There is a special blessing given to those who overcome by the blood of the Lamb (see Revelation 2:17). Jesus is still Savior of all men, but the question then becomes–when and at what point? This question will be answered in chapter 21.

Although Satan is legally destroyed, and has no lawful authority over the believer, God uses him as an opponent to train the Bride-elect in overcoming and in learning agape love. Thus when God our Father allows Satan to afflict one of His children (Bride-elect), it is not because Satan has any legal right to do so, but in order to train God's child in overcoming and in learning deeper dimensions of agape love.

Satan lost all of his claims at Calvary. Every child of God is legitimately delivered from all of his affliction and oppression. All that our Father permits to remain is only for training purposes. The Apostle Paul understood this when he said; *For our light affliction, which is but for a moment, is working for us a far more exceeding and eternal weight of glory...* 2 Corinthians 4:17. When anyone is delivered from affliction by faith here and now, he has triumphed. When the symptoms persist and he has learned a new dimension of agape love, he has also triumphed because he has increased his eternal rank!

In the final execution of God's judgment over Satan, it will be seen that no cause for the continuation of evil (sin and death) will exist. When God our Father demands of Satan; *"What legal rights do you have, as the father of all lies?"* The father of evil can render no excuse. Evil will have served its ultimate purpose, all to the glory and honor of God Almighty, who was, and is, and is yet to come! Amen.

20

God's Hidden Gifts To Us

If you never felt pain, how would you know that I am the Healer? If you never had difficulty, how would you know that I am the Deliverer? If you never made a mistake, how would you know that I am forgiving? If you never were broken, how would you know that I can make you whole? If you never went through the fire, then how would you become pure? If you had all power, then how would you learn to depend on Me? If your life were perfect, then what would you need Me for?

A man found a cocoon of a butterfly. One day a small opening appeared. He sat and watched the butterfly for several hours as it struggled to force its body through that little hole. Then it seemed to stop making any progress. It appeared as if it had gotten as far as it could, and go no further.

So the man decided to help the butterfly. He took a pair of scissors and snipped off the remaining bit of the cocoon. The butterfly then emerged easily. But it had a swollen body and small shriveled wings. The man continued to watch the butterfly because he expected that at any moment, the wings would enlarge and expand to be able to support the body, which would contract in time.

Neither happened! In fact, the butterfly spent the rest of its life crawling around with a swollen body and shriveled wings. It never was able to fly. What the man in his kindness and haste did not understand was that the restricting cocoon and the struggle were required for the butterfly. *To get through the tiny opening was God's way of forcing fluid from the body of the butterfly into its wings so that it would be ready for flight,* to achieve its freedom from the cocoon. Sometimes struggles are exactly what we need in our lives. If God allowed us to go through our lives without any obstacles, it would cripple us. We would not be as strong as we could have been. We could never fly!

I asked for strength... and God gave me difficulties to make me strong. I asked for wisdom... and God gave me problems to solve. I asked for prosperity... and God gave me brain and brawn to work. I asked for courage... and God gave me danger to overcome. I asked for love... and God gave me troubled people to help. I asked for favors... and God gave me opportunities. I received nothing I wanted... and God gave me everything I needed. No suffering = No throne. Know suffering = Know throne.

21

Depravity Of The Human Nature
And The Parable Of
The Rich Man And Lazarus

One of the most important aspects of God's eternal purpose for humanity is for her ultimate redemption from depravity (depravity will be more clearly defined a little further into this presentation). The incredible complexity of our earthly existence with all of its trials and tribulations, pain and suffering, will be redeemed for God's glorious eternal purpose by the sanctifying work of the Living Christ. The sanctifying work of Jesus Christ will finally bring all the families of God into the fullness of God's expression demonstrating that God's love for humanity never fails! *... Love never gives up, never loses faith, is always hopeful, and endures through every circumstance. Love will last forever, but prophecy and speaking in unknown languages and special knowledge will all disappear.*1 Corinthians 13:7, 8. NLT.

To bring clarity to the term; the fullness of God's expression, I would like to draw your attention to a passage of Scripture as found in Colossians 3:1-4; *Since you have been raised to new life with Christ, set your sights on the realities of Heaven, where Christ sits at God's right hand in the place of honour and power. Let Heaven fill your thoughts. Do not think only about things down here on earth. For you died when Christ died, and your real life is hidden with Christ in God. And when Christ, who is your real life, is revealed to the whole world, you will share in all His glory.* NLT

To bring clarity to the term; Sanctification as defined by Easton's Bible Dictionary, I **quote**; *Sanctification involves more than a mere moral reformation of character, brought about by the power of the truth: it is the work of Holy Spirit bringing the whole nature more and more under the influences of the new gracious principles implanted in the soul in regeneration. In other words, sanctification is the carrying on to perfection the work begun in regeneration, and it extends to the whole man (Romans 6:13; 2 Corinthians 4:6; Colossians 3:10; 1 John 4:7; 1 Corinthians 6:19). It is the special office of Holy Spirit in the plan of redemption to carry on this work (1 Corinthians 6:11; 2 Thessalonians 2:13). Faith is instrumental in securing sanctification, inasmuch as it secures union to Christ (Galatians 2:20), and brings the believer into living contact with the truth, whereby he is led to yield obedience "to the commands, trembling at the threatenings, and embracing the promises of God for this life and that which is to come." Perfect sanctification is not attainable in this life (1 Kings 8:46; Proverbs 20:9; Ecclesiastes 7:20; James 3:2; 1 John 1:8). See Paul's account of himself in Romans 7:14-25; Philippians 3:12-14; and 1 Timothy 1:15; also the confessions of David (Psalm 19:12,13; 51), of Moses (Psalm 90:8), of (Job 42:5,6), and of Daniel (Job 9:3-20). "The more holy a man is, the more humble, self-renouncing, self-abhorring, and the more sensitive to every sin he becomes, and the more closely he clings to Christ. The moral imperfections which cling to him he feels to be sins, which he laments and strives to overcome. Believers find that their life is a constant warfare, and they need to take the kingdom of Heaven by storm, and watch while they pray. They are always subject to the constant chastisement of their Father's loving hand, which can only be designed to correct their imperfections and to confirm their graces. And it has been notoriously the fact that the best Christians* *have been those who have been the least prone to claim the attainment of perfection for themselves* (**Hodge's Outlines**) **End of quote**.

According to Scripture, our real lives are hidden in Christ. By God's sovereign choosing, the mystery of His eternal purpose for humanity was not revealed to the world in any of the earlier ages of time. However, at the appointed fullness of time, God chose to reveal the mystery of His eternal purpose for humanity through His Son Jesus the Christ ...*But when the fullness of the time had come, God sent forth His Son, born of a woman, born under the law, to redeem those who were under the law, that we might receive the adoption as sons.* Galatians 4:4, 5.

For since by man came death, by Man also came the resurrection of the dead. For as in Adam all die, even so in Christ all shall be made alive. But each one in his own order: Christ the firstfruits, afterward those who are Christ's at His coming. Then comes the end, when He delivers the kingdom to God the Father, when He puts an end to all rule and all authority and power. For He must reign until He has put all enemies under His feet. The last enemy that will be destroyed is death. 1 Corinthians 15:20-26.

The fullness that all of humanity will eventually enjoy will be in the sharing of God's glory! Ultimately this brings about our completeness that can only be found in the finished work of Christ. There is however, an order to our redemption and restoration.

T. Austin Sparks[4] in one of his writings says, **I quote;** *"God always begins from completeness. He has everything in Himself fully and finally–before He makes a beginning, and all His subsequent activities are really working backward to fullness, although to man they appear to be the new things of God. The course then has been that God begins with fullness. Man falls away and loses that fullness. Then God reacts and steadily moves in progressive and gradual recovery of that fullness."* **End of quote.**

I believe that our great God and Savior allowed humanity

to fall away from fullness so that in and through Christ and in due time and season, we could gradually recover to fullness with a deeper, richer, and purer understanding of whom Father God, Holy Spirit, and Jesus Christ are in their eternality! Through many trials and tribulations, eventually we are brought back to fullness through the work of sanctification.

No matter how free we believe ourselves to be, as long as we have breath to breathe, we will continue to experience times of testing's that are always under God's control regardless of who we are. These experiences are critical for our ultimate eternal perfection! If this were not so, then there would be no point for any of us to experience the process of reconditioning (redeeming restoration) through the sanctifying work of the Living Christ.

Before we as individuals can begin to experience God's never failing love, grace, mercy and forgiveness through the sanctifying work of the Living Christ, personal illumination regarding our carnality and the depravity of our nature due to our sinful condition is absolutely necessary.

The seeds of original sin can be traced back to within the hearts and minds (souls) of Adam and Eve. Temptation was introduced to Adam and Eve from an external influence (Satan). Through temptation, Adam and Eve fell, causing them to be lowered into the realm of carnality and depravity. When those seeds took root and began to grow, it would only be a matter of time for a strange, but lethal new way of reasoning to be entertained by them.

According to Noah Webster's New International Dictionary of the English Language the word Carnality is defined as: *1. (a.) Sensual; pertaining to the body or its appetites; fleshly; sensual; human or worldly as opposed to spiritual. 2. (a.) Flesh-devouring; cruel; ravenous; bloody. This refers to the flesh as opposed to the "spirit," and denotes, in an ethical sense, mere human nature, the lower side of man as apart from the Divine influence, and therefore estranged from God and prone to sin; whatever in the soul that is found to be weak leans toward ungodliness.*

Depravity is defined as: *(n.) The state of being depraved or corrupted; a vitiated state of moral character; general badness of character; wickedness of mind or heart; absence of religious feeling and principle.*

The consequence of Adam and Eve's sinful desires (desires they thought to be good at first), gave them their independence. Painfully their independence separated them from God spiritually, eventually leading to their physical death. Their sin nature was passed down through their genetics (spiritual D.N.A.) to all of their posterity, (excluding Jesus Christ, the perfect God-man) affecting all of humankind to this day.

Thank God that carnality and depravity will never be able to stop our heavenly Father from reaching into our darkest realms of existence with His never failing love. His corrective judgments ultimately are loving, kind and just! The very nature of God's love for humanity goes far beyond our natural comprehension and understanding! His sovereign mercies are new every day. Please consider; Psalm 139:1-18.

O Lord, You have examined my heart and know everything about me. You know when I sit down or stand up. You know my every thought when far away. You chart the path ahead of me and tell me where to stop and rest. Every moment you know where I am. You know what I am going to say even before I say it, Lord. You both precede and follow me. You place your hand of blessing on my head. Such knowledge is too wonderful for me, too great for me to know! I can never escape from Your spirit! I can never get away from Your presence! If I go up to Heaven, You are there; if I go down to the place of the dead, You are there. If I ride the wings of the morning, if I dwell by the farthest oceans, even there Your hand will guide me, and Your strength will support me. I could ask the darkness to hide me and the light around me to become night–but even in darkness I cannot hide from You. To You the night shines as bright as day. Darkness and light are both alike to You. You made all the delicate, inner parts of my body and knit me together in my mother's womb. Thank You for making me so wonderfully complex! Your workmanship is marvelous—and how well I know it. You saw me before I was born. Every day of my life was recorded in Your book. Every moment was laid out before a single day had passed. How precious are Your thoughts about me, O God! They are innumerable! I can't even count them; they outnumber the grains of sand! And when I wake up in the morning, You are still with me! NLT.

2 Timothy 1:9, 10. *It is God who saved us and chose us to live a Holy life. He did this not because we deserved it, but because that was His plan long before the world began – to show His love and kindness to us through Christ Jesus. And now He has made all of this plain to us by the coming of Christ Jesus, our Savior, who broke the power of death and showed us the way to everlasting life through the Good News.* NLT.

22

Undeserved Mercy

Every imaginable form of evil that can be contrived in the heart of man, from the subtle to the most horrific comes from within man's depraved soul realm. No one is exempt from the effects of carnality (sin) and how it infiltrates our lives. From the very young to the sweetest of the elderly, we are all capable of committing horrific deeds including murder and God only knows what else! Somehow we may think that we are better than the next person, when in fact, we could very well be that next person. If you don't believe this, just turn on the daily news. Without God's divine intervention and mercy, it would be impossible for any of us to be reconciled back to Him on the strength of our own merit, due to our inherited sin nature (total depravity).

Whatever limited free will choices that we are able to make in this life, will never bring us back to Him fully. Our choices will always be limited to within the confines of our own carnality and depravity. I believe that this is probably one of the most difficult concepts for any of us to accept. Another very difficult concept to accept is the idea that God purposed humanity to be lowered into the realm of carnality so that we could learn profound truths of His unfailing love, grace, mercy, and forgiveness that could not be learned otherwise without such contrasted demonstration.

These truths can only be learned through affliction,

suffering, and testing. Personal pride makes it nearly impossible for us to accept these facts, because we so desperately want to be the ones in control. Please consider Matthew 4:15,16; *In the land of Zebulun and of Naphtali, beside the sea, beyond the Jordan River–in Galilee where so many Gentiles live–the people who sat in darkness have seen a great Light. And for those who lived in the land where death casts its shadow, a Light has shined. From then on, Jesus began to preach, "Turn from your sins and turn to God, because the Kingdom of Heaven is near."* NLT.

Controlling pride (depravity) kept the people from Zebulun and Naphtali in darkness. They were not just living in darkness; they were sitting in it presumably unconcerned. Not only were they unconcerned, they were also living in the shadow of death un-aware. It took outside intervention, the Light of Jesus, and His teaching to change them. Please consider Ecclesiastes 3:11; *God has made everything beautiful for its own time. He has planted eternity in the human heart, but even so, people cannot see the whole scope of God's work from beginning to end.* NLT; Ecclesiastes 6:10. *Everything has already been decided. It was known long ago what each person would be. So there's no use arguing with God about your destiny.* NLT; Proverbs 16:33. *We may throw the dice, but the Lord determines how they fall.* NLT; Proverbs 19:21. *You can make many plans, but the lord's purpose will prevail.* NLT; Ecclesiastes 12:7. *For then the dust will return to the earth, and the spirit will return to God who gave it.* NLT; Romans 8:18-25. *Yet what we suffer now is nothing compared to the glory He will give us later. For all creation is waiting eagerly for that future day when God will reveal who His children really are. Against its will, all of creation was subjected to God's curse. But with eager hope, the creation looks forward to the day when it will join God's children in glorious freedom from death and decay. For we know that all creation has been groaning as in the pains of childbirth right up to the present time. And we believers also groan, even though we have the Holy Spirit within us as a foretaste of future glory, for we long for our bodies to be released from sin and suffering. We, too, wait with eager hope for the day when God will give us our full rights as His adopted children, including the new bodies He has promised us. We were given this hope when we were saved. If we already have something, we don't need to hope for it. Now that we are saved, we eagerly look forward to this freedom. For if you already have something, you don't need to hope for it. But if we look forward to something we don't yet have, we must wait patiently and confidently.* NLT; Romans 3:23. *For all have sinned; all fall short of God's glorious standard.* NLT; 2 Corinthians 4:4. *In their case the god of this world has blinded the minds of the unbelievers, to keep them from seeing the light of the gospel of the glory of Christ, who is the image of God.*NAS; Romans 3:9-12. *Well then, are we Jews better than others? No, not at all, for we have already shown that all people, whether Jews or Gentiles, are under the power of sin. As the Scriptures say, "No one is good–not even one. No one has real understanding; no one is seeking God."* NLT; Romans 8:20. *Against its will, everything on earth was subjected to God's curse.* NLT; Romans 11:32. *For God has imprisoned all people in their own disobedience so He could have mercy on everyone.* NLT; John 6:43-45. *But Jesus replied, "Don't complain about what I said. For people can't come to Me unless the Father who sent Me draws them to Me, and at the last day I will raise them from the dead. As it is written in the Scriptures, "They will all be taught by God." Everyone who hears and learns from the Father comes to Me.* NLT; John 10:16. *I have other sheep, too, that are not in this sheepfold. I must bring them also, and they will listen to My voice; and there will be one flock with one shepherd.* NLT.

With this understanding, and with a willingness to genuinely repent and turn from our sinful ways (rebellion) by admission and through confession, we will begin to experience God's forgiveness, grace and mercy through His unfailing love. God's grace and mercy is not cheap, it cost Him dearly. We also have a price to pay. Dying to self (our carnal nature) and to the ways of the world with all of its temporal pleasures and temptations is no easy task. Our only hope of ever being victorious over sin and death is by the intervening work of Holy Spirit through the crucified life of Jesus Christ and His resurrection from the dead.

In Matthew 7:13, 14 Jesus says; *"Enter by the narrow gate; for wide is the gate and broad is the way that leads to destruction, and there are many who go in by it. Because narrow is the gate and difficult is the way which leads to life, and there are few who find it."*

23

Have You Heard The Good News?

Genuine repentance can only come about if one is first able to hear the good news message of the gospel of Jesus Christ, and then have opportunity to respond to the message. I have often wondered how billions of countless souls that have ever lived on planet earth, could be condemned and eternally separated from the love of God, if they have never been given the opportunity to hear the gospel message of salvation. There must be something extraordinary going on in the supernatural spiritual realm concerning reconciliation and restoration other than what we have been led to believe by leading theologians and Bible commentators. ... *Anyone who calls on the name of the Lord will be saved. But how can they call on Him to save them unless they believe in Him? And how can they believe in Him if they have never heard about Him? And how can they hear about Him unless someone tells them? And how will anyone go and tell them without being sent? That is what the Scriptures mean when they say, "How beautiful are the feet of those who bring good news!"* Romans 10:13-15. NLT.

For those who have heard the good news message of the gospel in this life, but then reject the message by deliberately choosing not to believe the truth of the message, are actually coming against the prompting of Holy Spirit. I must emphasize the importance in saying that I personally do believe that

God's judgment will be over that person for as long as they remain in unbelief.

I would like to quote to you a paragraph concerning God's judgment taken from a book titled, God's Plan For All.[5] The book was written by David and Zoe Sulem, a Christian married couple living in England. The book is available as a free download from their web site.

David and Zoe have some very profound insight into the Great White Throne judgment of God that is consistent with the truth of God's Holy Word, and something that I personally am strongly in agreement with. **I quote;** *The Millennial Age will be followed by the Great White Throne Judgment Age when all resurrected unbelievers will experience God's refining yet merciful Lake of Fire Judgment. Yes, it is appointed for men to die once and after that comes judgment, but this is not a judgment to torture people forever in Hell. Traditional Christianity has failed to understand that God's Lake of Fire Judgment will be corrective and it will flow out of God's love and His mercy to lead unbelievers to repentance and faith in Jesus Christ, who died for the sins of the whole world. The Elect Bride, united and working together with the Lord of the Harvest, will play a vital role as laborers to evangelize and reap the Great Harvest of abundant fruits of the rest of humanity, yet to be saved in the Millennial Age and the Great White Throne Judgment Age. Ultimately, in God's time and order, all people will be saved and reconciled to God through the shed blood of Jesus Christ on the cross. All people without exception will freely and thankfully enter the Eternal Kingdom of God of the New Heaven and the New Earth.* **End of quotation.**

I realize that some of you may be asking the question, What about the unpardonable sin of blasphemy against Holy Spirit? If blasphemy against Holy Spirit is unpardonable, then what exactly is blasphemy? Excellent question, let's look at some definitions of this word as found in Easton's Bible Dictionary; **I quote;** *The word blasphemy in one sense refers to speaking evil of God. This word is found in Psalm 74:18; Isaiah 52:5;*

Romans 2:24; Revelation 13:1, 6; 16:9, 11, 21. It denotes also any kind of calumny, or evil-speaking, or abuse (1 Kings 21:10; Acts 13:45; 18:6, etc.). Our Lord was accused of blasphemy when He claimed to be the Son of God (Matthew 26:65; Matthew 9:3; Mark 2:7). They who deny His Messiahship blaspheme Jesus (Luke 22:65; John 10:36). Blasphemy against the Holy Ghost (Matthew 12:31, 32; Mark 3:28, 29; Luke 12:10) is regarded by some as a continued and obstinate rejection of the gospel, and hence is an unpardonable sin, simply because as long as a sinner remains in unbelief he voluntarily excludes himself from pardon. Others regard the expression as designating the sin of attributing to the power of Satan those miracles which Christ performed, or generally those works which are the result of the Spirit's agency. **End of quotation.**

It is absolutely correct in saying that the unpardonable sin is the sin of unbelief. As long as a person is in a state of unbelief, there can be no true forgiveness of sin, thus perpetuating his/her condition. In essence the sin of unbelief is denying or not believing in the atoning work of Jesus Christ or in His deity as God the Savior.(God manifesting in the flesh as the perfect prototype man, the second Adam).

When the unbelieving person dies, we assume that their fate is sealed for all of eternity because that is what we have been traditionally taught to believe. What we fail to realize is that the king of Glory has power over physical and spiritual death, and the grave. The king of Glory can change the most hardened heart. Not only does He hold the keys to the ancient gates of His Father's Holy temple, He also holds the keys to the gates of Hades.

Who is this King of Glory? *Open up, ancient gates! Open up, ancient doors, and let the King of glory enter. Who is the King of glory? The Lord, strong and mighty, the Lord, invincible in battle. Open up, ancient gates! Open up, ancient doors, and let the King of glory enter. Who is the King of glory? The Lord Almighty–He is the King of glory.* Psalm 24; 7-10.

There are certain aspects of God's judgment that He has chosen not to completely reveal to us through Scripture, so for the most part, we can only speculate. For example, a Scripture passage found in 1 Peter 4:6 says; *For this reason the gospel was preached also to those who are dead, that they might be judged according to men in the flesh, but live according to God in the spirit.* What exactly does this Scripture passage mean? Or, what exactly does Scripture mean to say in Romans 10:10? *...For with the heart one believes unto righteousness, and with the mouth confession is made unto salvation.*

I believe Scripture teaches that eventually the scales will be removed from the eyes of all unbelievers by the King of Glory when they see the one whom they have pierced standing in the midst of the flame. The very flame they find themselves to be in!I am certain that the majority of those who are familiar with Scripture will be outraged with such apparent heresy! You are probably already asking the question; What about the rich man and Lazarus as found in Luke 16:19-31? Let us examine this parable as follows; *Jesus said, "There was a certain rich man who was splendidly clothed and who lived each day in luxury. At his door lay a diseased beggar named Lazarus. As Lazarus lay there longing for scraps from the rich man's table, the dogs would come and lick his open sores. Finally, the beggar died and was carried by the angels to be with Abraham. The rich man also died and was buried, and his soul went to the place of the dead (Hell). There, in torment, he saw Lazarus in the far distance with Abraham. The rich man shouted, Father Abraham, have some pity! Send Lazarus over here to dip the tip of his finger in water and cool my tongue, because I am in anguish in these flames. But Abraham said to him, Son, remember that during your lifetime you had everything you wanted, and Lazarus had nothing. So now he is here being comforted, and you are in anguish. And besides, there is a great chasm separating us. Anyone who wanted to cross over to you from here is stopped at its edge, and no one there can cross over to us. Then the rich man said, Please, Father Abraham, send him to my father's home. For I have five brothers, and I want him to warn them about this place of torment so they won't have to come here when they die. But*

Abraham said, Moses and the prophets have warned them. Your brothers can read their writings anytime they want to. The rich man replied, No, Father Abraham! But if someone is sent to them from the dead, then they will turn from their sins. But Abraham said, If they won't listen to Moses and the prophets, they won't listen even if someone rises from the dead." NLT.

A few obvious things that we can pick up in this parable are; 1.) There is a place for the dead; 2.) There is a place of torment within the flame; 3.) There is a great chasm that no man can cross; 4.) No communication or warning possible between the living and the dead.

One of the first questions that came to my mind concerning the rich man who was found to be in the place of the dead was; who qualifies in every possible way to help the rich man? A man named Abraham? I don't think so! Abraham doesn't hold the keys to death and the grave. However, there is one who does. His name is Jesus the Christ! Let's look at Revelation 1:17, 18.

And when I saw Him, I fell at His feet as dead. But He laid His right hand on me, saying to me, "Do not be afraid; I am the First and the Last. I am He who lives, and was dead, and behold, I am alive forevermore. Amen. And I have the keys of Hades and of Death.

This verse can be confirmed with 1 Peter 4:5, 6 reading as follows; *But just remember that they will have to face God, who will judge everyone, both the living and the dead. That is why the Good News was preached even to those who have died– so that although their bodies were punished with death, they could still live in the spirit as God does.* NLT.

Again, David and Zoe Sulem have profoundly important things to share with us from their book; "God's Plan For All." It is with their express permission that I quote to you the entire chapter 19 of "God's Plan For All." **I quote;** *The parable of the rich man and Lazarus, as given in* Luke 16:19-31, *speaks about the mystery of the Kingdom of God. This parable is the most misunderstood parable of all of Jesus' parables.*

Unfortunately, many Christians read this parable as if it was a true literal account, and this is why they misapply and misunderstand the spiritual truths about the Kingdom of God conveyed by Jesus. This is despite a clear biblical statement made by Jesus telling us that He never spoke to the multitudes except in parables when conveying spiritual truths.

Matthew 13:10-11; *And the disciples came and said to Him, "Why do You speak to them in parables?" He answered and said to them, "Because it has been given to you to know the mysteries of the kingdom of Heaven, but to them it has not been given.*

Notice that the Kingdom of Heaven, which means the same as the Kingdom of God, has mysteries, and only Christ's disciples are meant to understand them. Jesus Christ spoke in parables to hide the meaning of the mysteries of the Kingdom of God from unbelievers. Matthew 13:34-35; *All these things Jesus spoke to the multitude in parables; and without a parable He did not speak to them, that it might be fulfilled which was spoken by the prophet, saying: "I will open My mouth in parables; I will utter things kept secret from the foundation of the world."*

Notice that the mysteries of the Kingdom of God were kept secret from people from the foundation of the world. Apostle Paul was one of the first among the early apostles to whom God clearly revealed all aspects of the mystery of the Kingdom of God hidden in Jesus' parables, including the parable of the rich man and Lazarus.

Ephesians 3:1-6; *For this reason I, Paul, the prisoner of Christ Jesus for you Gentiles–if indeed you have heard of the dispensation of the grace of God which was given to me for you, how that by revelation He made known to me the mystery (as I have briefly written already, by which, when you read, you may understand my knowledge in the mystery of Christ), which (the mystery) in other ages was not made known to the sons of men, as it has now been revealed by the Spirit to His holy apostles and prophets: that the Gentiles should be fellow heirs, and of the same body, and partakers* of His promise in Christ by the gospel.

An important aspect of the mystery of the Kingdom of God is that the Gentiles are fellow heirs with the Israelites. Jews and especially the self-righteous Pharisees looked down on the Gentiles, considering them as cut off from the Kingdom of God. The truth that the Gentiles are fellow heirs with the Jews in the Kingdom of God was an important revelation to Paul, who had been a self-righteous Pharisee, before his conversion to Christianity.

Romans 11:25-27; *For I do not desire, brethren, that you should be ignorant of this mystery, lest you should be wise in your own opinion, that blindness in part has happened to Israel until the fullness of the Gentiles has come in. And so all Israel will be saved, as it is written: "The Deliverer will come out of Zion, and He will turn away ungodliness from Jacob; for this is My covenant with them, when I take away their sins."*

This is a key Scripture to understand the parable of the rich man and Lazarus and the mystery of the Kingdom of God. Here, Apostle Paul urges us not to be ignorant of two important aspects of the mystery of the Kingdom of God.

Firstly, God has purposely blinded a part of Israel, actually most of Israel, from believing the gospel of Christ until the full number of Gentile Elect have come to Christ before they die. Secondly, all Israel will be saved when the Deliverer will come to Jerusalem. This undoubtedly refers to the Second Coming of Jesus Christ, when He returns to establish His Millennial Kingdom of God. All Israel means absolutely all Israel without exception, past, present and future. It is a shame that most Christians remain ignorant of this important aspect of the mystery of the Kingdom of God that God's purpose is ultimately to save all Israel. This is also good news for all Gentiles, because all Gentiles will also be saved by the Seed of Abraham, the King of the Jews, who is Jesus Christ.

Let us remind ourselves of how God will save all Israel. God will first save a remnant of Israel together with the full number of Gentile Elect at the Second Coming of Jesus Christ. These are all those who have been called and chosen both from Israel and the Gentile nations, who are God's Elect and they will be raised up as the Bride of Christ when Jesus comes again. Then, in the Millennial Kingdom of God, all surviving Jews and all Jews born throughout the Millennial Age will be saved before they die. Finally, following the Millennial Age, during the Great White Throne Judgment Age, all remaining unbelieving Jews will be resurrected and saved, but as through fire in the Lake of Fire. This will fulfill God's covenant to save all Israel, thus taking away their sins.

Romans Chapters 11 *is an important chapter where God reveals to Apostle Paul that all unbelieving Israelites are not permanently rejected by God and that His purpose is ultimately to save all Israel. This subject is covered in detail in Chapter 7 "God's Purpose for Israel." We are only able to understand the parable of the rich man and Lazarus once we have the revelation of the mystery of the Kingdom of God, as discussed above. Now let us study the parable.* Luke 16:19-31; *There was a certain rich man who was clothed in purple and fine linen and fared sumptuously every day. But there was a certain beggar named Lazarus, full of sores, who was laid at his gate, desiring to be fed with the crumbs which fell from the rich man's table. Moreover the dogs came and licked his sores. So it was that the beggar died, and was carried by the angels to Abraham's bosom. The rich man also died and was buried. And being in torments in Hades, he lifted up his eyes and saw Abraham afar off, and Lazarus in his bosom. Then he cried and said, 'Father Abraham, have mercy on me, and send Lazarus that he may dip the tip of his finger in water and cool my tongue; for I am tormented in this flame.' But Abraham said, 'Son, remember that in your lifetime you received your good things, and likewise Lazarus evil things; but now he is comforted and you are tormented. And besides all this, between us and you there is a great gulf fixed, so that those who want to pass from here to you cannot, nor can those from there pass to us.' Then he said, 'I beg you therefore, father, that you would send him to my father's house, for I have five brothers that he may testify to them, lest they also come to this place of torment.' Abraham said to him, 'They have Moses and the prophets; let them hear them.' And he said, 'No, father Abraham; but if one goes to them from the dead, they will repent.' But he said to him, 'If they do not hear Moses and the prophets, neither will they be persuaded though one rise from the dead.'*

The purpose of this parable is to confirm several aspects of the spiritual truths of the mystery of the Kingdom of God revealed elsewhere in the Bible. The first thing we need to understand is that the rich man and Lazarus are two ficti-tious characters who represent two groups of real people. It is important to identify who these two groups of people are.

The rich man calls Abraham, Father Abraham, and Abraham calls him son, in verses 24 and 25 above. It is clear that the rich man is an Israelite, a direct physical descendant of Abraham through the spiritually rich line of Isaac and Jacob. The rich man represents all unbelieving Israelites who are olive branches that have been temporarily cut off from their own natural spiritually rich and royal Holy Olive Tree of Israel. (Romans 11:16-17)

Let us now understand that Lazarus represents all of the Gentile Elect, who are naturally wild olive branches that are now grafted into the spiritually rich Holy Olive Tree of Israel. (Romans 11:19) *The story of Jesus dealing with the Gentile Canaanite woman in* Matthew 15:21-28, *gives us the revela-tion of the identity of Lazarus as a Gentile Elect.*

Matthew 15:21-28; *Then Jesus went out from there and departed to the region of Tyre and Sidon. And behold, a woman of Canaan came from that region and cried out to Him, saying, "Have mercy on me, O Lord, Son of David! My daughter is severely demon-possessed." But He answered her not a word. And His disciples came and urged Him, saying, "Send her away, for she cries out after us." 24 But He answered and said, "I was not sent except to the lost sheep of the house of Israel." Then she came and worshiped Him, saying, "Lord, help me!" But He answered and said, "It is not good yet even the little dogs eat the crumbs which fall from their masters' table." Then Jesus answered and said to her, "O woman, great is your faith! Let it be to you as you desire." And her daughter was healed from that very hour.*

This is not a parable, but a true story of a Canaanite woman who was a Gentile believer. She was one of God's Elect, and had great God given faith to believe as a true worshiper of Jesus Christ. She had an amazingly humble spirit, in great contrast to the self-righteous and proud Pharisees. Pharisees looked down upon Gentiles as dogs and Jesus Christ used the same terminology to test the faith of this Gentile woman. She was willing to be a spiritual beggar and wanted every crumb of blessing she could get from Jesus, as she understood her total dependence upon Him, the Savior of Israel, for her daughter's healing.

In the parable of the rich man and Lazarus, Jesus Christ used the name Lazarus to denote a Gentile believer. The name Lazarus is a form of the Hebrew name Eliezer as confirmed in Strong's number G2976. Eliezer was a Gentile faithful servant of Abraham, whom God used to get a bride for Isaac. (Genesis 15:2, 24:1-66)

The description and attitude of Lazarus in the parable resemble that of the Gentile Canaanite woman. Like her, Lazarus is associated with dogs, and he is also a spiritual beggar dependent on the crumbs that fell from the rich man's table. Lazarus also understood that his spiritual hunger could only be satisfied through the spiritually rich Abrahamic blessing given to the Jews, and ultimately through the Seed of Abraham, who is Jesus Christ himself, the Bread of Life.

The first point to note from the parable of the rich man and Lazarus is the revelation of the spiritual truth that unbelieving Israelites have been temporarily broken off from their own spiritually rich natural Holy Olive Tree of Israel. This has happened in order to fulfill God's will to graft into the Holy Olive Tree of Israel, a set number of wild olive branches who are God's Gentile Elect. (Romans 11:16-20)

All unbelieving Israelites (the cut off natural olive branches) will miss out on the first phase of the Kingdom of

God, which is the Millennial Kingdom of Jesus Christ on this earth. However, Apostle Paul makes it abundantly clear in Romans Chapter 11 that God has not permanently rejected unbelieving Israelites, and ultimately His Plan is to save all Israel.

Luke 16:22; *So it was that the beggar died, and was carried by the angels to Abraham's bosom... In this verse, Lazarus after his death is pictured in Abraham's bosom. This is a beautiful spiritual picture of a Gentile believer grafted into the spiritually rich Holy Olive Tree of Israel represented by Abraham, the Father of the Jewish nation, to whom the Covenant to bless all the families of the earth was given (Genesis 12:2-3). Let us continue to understand the spiritual truths revealed in this parable.*

Luke 16:22-23; *...The rich man also died and was buried. And being in torments (basanos) in Hades, he lifted up his eyes and saw Abraham afar off, and Lazarus in his bosom. The verses above prove that the story of the rich man and Lazarus is a parable and not a true factual account. It would be ridiculous to think that billions of dead unbelievers are able to lift up their eyes from their graves (hades) and see Abraham and believers like Lazarus in Abraham's bosom. The powerful truth of the Bible is that when a person dies, he 'sleeps' and remains unconscious until his resurrection.*

Note that it does not say that Lazarus' spirit or his soul went to Heaven nor does it say that the rich man's spirit or his soul went to Hell. One cannot use the Scripture above to prove that when a person dies, his soul is immediately judged by God to go to Heaven or Hell. In the previous chapter, we have explained the biblical truth that people are not born with immortal souls, and after death, they remain in an unconscious 'sleep' until their resurrection.

Also, let us remind ourselves of the meaning of the Greek word basanos, which has been translated as torment in Luke 16:23 *quoted above. According to Strong's number G931, the primary meaning of basanos is to test (metals) by the touchstone, which is a black siliceous stone used to test the purity of gold or silver by the color of the streak produced on it by rubbing it with either metal. The use of the Greek word basanos indicates that there is a refining judgment awaiting the rich man after his resurrection and not eternal torment.*

We know that nobody can be tormented in Hades (the grave), as the Bible is very clear about what happens when people die. The Bible says that all dead people remain in an unconscious 'sleep' in their graves until their resurrection. Please remember that the rich man and Lazarus story is a parable and not a true account. The purpose of this parable is to hide the mysteries of the Kingdom of God from unbelievers and it is not intended to be understood as an actual event.

Luke 16:24; *Then he cried and said, 'Father Abraham, have mercy on me, and send Lazarus that he may dip the tip of his finger in water and cool my tongue; for I am tormented in this flame.'*

This powerful and wonderful verse proves that an unbelieving Jew, after his death, will repent and plead for God's mercy when he is judged in God's refining Lake of Fire, during the Great White Throne Judgment Age.

The rich man humbly accepts that it is Lazarus the Gentile, rather than him, who is connected into the spiritually rich Holy Olive Tree of Israel, and it is Lazarus who has access to the Living Water flowing from the Seed of Abraham, Jesus Christ Himself. The rich man further understands and knows that even one drop of water, given to him by Lazarus who has access to the Living Water of Life, is sufficient to satisfy his spiritual thirst.

Apostle Paul says that God's purpose to save the Gentile Elect before most of the Jews will provoke these unbelieving Jews to jealousy. (Romans 11:11) *This will be holy jealousy provoking them to desire the same Living Water accessed by God's Gentile Elect. Apostle Paul further says that it is through the Gentile Elect that God will show mercy to the unbelieving Jews, and ultimately all Jews will receive God's mercy.*(Romans11:30-32)

The attitude of the rich man in Hades, after his death,

wonderfully compares with the attitude of Lazarus in life, before his death.

Before death, all Gentile Elect believers, represented by Lazarus, will repent and humble themselves to become spiritual beggars. They will believe through God given faith and understand that even the crumbs, which fall from the rich man's table, are sufficient to satisfy their spiritual hunger, because these crumbs represent the Bread of Life promised to the Jewish nation through the Abrahamic Covenant. Of course, the Bread of Life is Jesus Christ himself, who is the Seed of Abraham.

After death, all unbelieving Israelites, represented by the rich man, will humble themselves to become spiritual beggars just like Lazarus before he died. All unbelieving Israelites who are cut off from their Holy Olive Tree, and who will be resurrected at the Second Resurrection, will repent and plead for God's mercy in God's refining yet merciful Lake of Fire judgment. They will understand through God given faith that even a drop of Living Water from 'Lazarus' is sufficient to satisfy their spiritual thirst. They will know that this Living Water is Jesus Christ Himself, the Seed of Abraham.

Luke 16:24 above, makes complete nonsense of the traditional view of Hell, which says that a dead unbeliever is permanently cut off from communicating with God and that he has no possibility of coming to genuine repentance.

Luke 16:25; But Abraham said, 'Son, remember that in your lifetime you received your good things, and likewise Lazarus evil things; but now he is comforted and you are tormented.' This verse refers to the spiritually false self-exalting view of unbelieving Israelites who consider themselves as spiritually rich and the Gentiles as spiritually poor. The truth of the matter is quite the opposite. It is unbelieving Israelites who are spiritually very poor because they are broken off from their rich Holy Olive Tree of Israel. It is the believing Gentiles who are spiritually very rich, as they are grafted into the Holy Olive Tree of Israel and have therefore benefited because of the broken off Jewish branches.

Again, this verse makes nonsense of the traditional view of Hell, which says that God's love for unbelievers ends after death. Please note, that Abraham has a loving and caring approach towards the rich man shown by Abraham calling him son.

Luke 16:26; *And besides all this, between us and you there is a great gulf fixed, so that those who want to pass from here to you cannot, nor can those from there pass to us.'*

The great gulf spoken of in this verse is the great gulf of the thousand-year Millennial Kingdom Age. This verse is not speaking about a permanent eternal gulf of unbelief and separation between Lazarus and the rich man. The gulf will be bridged when the rich man is resurrected in his immortal body in the Second Resurrection, at the end of the thousand-year Millennial Kingdom of Jesus Christ. This is when he will face God's refining judgment in the Lake of Fire and repent and be saved.

Luke 16:27-30; *Then he said, 'I beg you therefore, father, that you would send him to my father's house, for I have five brothers, that he may testify to them, lest they also come to this place of torment.' Abraham said to him, 'They have Moses and the prophets; let them hear them.' And he said, 'No, father Abraham; but if one goes to them from the dead, they will repent.'*

The rich man shows love and concern for his brothers, fellow Israelites who remain as unbelievers. Apostle Paul also had great love and concern for his fellow Israelites who remained unbelievers. The verses above also show that the rich man understands the importance of genuine repentance before death, in order for his fellow Israelites not to have to face God's refining judgment in the Lake of Fire.

Luke 16:31; *But he said to him, 'If they do not hear Moses and the prophets, neither will they be persuaded though one rise from the dead.'*

This verse refers to the Law of Moses and to the resurrection of Jesus Christ. Jews cannot be saved through keeping the Law of Moses or even if they personally witness or hear of the miracle of Jesus Christ rising from the dead. This verse demonstrates the powerful truth of Election by Grace. Salvation is entirely a matter of God's Will. A person can only come to Jesus and be saved if the Father draws him to Jesus, and every person whom the Father draws will come to Jesus (John 6:37, 44).

Ultimately, it is God's purpose to draw all people from darkness into the light of Jesus Christ. All Israel, as well as all Gentiles, will be saved in God's time and His order.

Corinthians 15:22-23; *For as in Adam all die, even so in Christ all shall be made alive. But each one in his own order.*

Conclusion: There are three important spiritual truths about the Kingdom of God hidden in the parable of the rich man and Lazarus. We believe the time has come for God to clearly reveal these spiritual truths to His Elect, before the Second Coming of Jesus Christ. These spiritual truths are: 1) After death and following the First Resurrection, Gentile believers, God's Elect represented by Lazarus, will be rewarded with the blessing of Abraham, which is to enter into the Millennial Kingdom of Jesus Christ because they are fully connected into the Holy Olive Tree of Israel. 2) After death and following the Second Resurrection, all unbelieving Israelites represented by the rich man, will go through God's refining, corrective judgment in the Lake of Fire, where they will repent and be grafted back into their natural Holy Olive Tree of Israel. This will fulfill God's covenant with Abraham to save all Israel. 3) The powerful truth of Election by Grace: No Jew can be saved through the Law of Moses or through the writings of the Old Testament prophets, or even through witnessing or hearing about the miracle of the resurrection of Jesus Christ. Salvation is entirely a matter of God's Will, which He is carrying out in His own time and order. Ultimately, all people without exception will be reconciled to God through God given gifts of repentance and faith in the sacrifice of Jesus Christ who died for the sins of the whole world. **End of quoted chapter.**

What no man is capable of doing, Jesus Christ the King of

Glory is fully capable of doing, because He holds the keys to death and the grave Alleluia!

Those who have been blinded from this truth or those who have had their hearts hardened, will at some point come to believe, because of God's irresistible grace (keys that Jesus holds) working on their behalf. According to Philippians 2:10,11 it says; *"That at the name of Jesus every knee should bow, of those in Heaven, and of those on earth, and of those under the earth, and that every tongue should confess that Jesus Christ is Lord, to the glory of God the Father."* There are those who would have us believe that many will be forced to bow before God with seared consciences and a sealed fate of eternal doom. But this belief is unscriptural. Forced adoration with a seared conscience while on bended knee before almighty God serves no purpose and goes against God's redeeming nature, because the very essence of God is pure unfailing love!

The International Standard Bible Encyclopedia defines to bow on bended knee as follows, **I quote;** *To Bow In Adoration: To Bow in adoration is intense admiration culminating in reverence and worship, together with the outward acts and attitudes which accompany such reverence. It thus includes both the subjective sentiments, or feelings of the soul, in the presence of some superior object or person, and the appropriate physical expressions of such sentiments in outward acts of homage or of worship. But it finds its highest expression in religion. To bow in adoration is perhaps the highest type of worship, involving the reverent and rapt contemplation of the Divine perfections and prerogatives, the acknowledgment of them in words of praise, together with the visible symbols and postures that express the adoring attitude of the creature in the presence of his Creator. It is the expression of the soul's mystical realization of God's presence in His transcendent greatness, Holiness and loving-kindness. As a form of prayer, adoration is to be distinguished from other forms, such as petition, thanksgiving, confession and intercession. In the Old Testament and New Testament, these* *are similar to those which prevailed in all oriental countries, as amply illustrated by the monuments of Egypt and Assyria, and by the customs still in use among the nations of the East. The chief attitudes referred to in the Bible are the following: 1.Prostration: Among the Orientals, especially Persians, prostration (i.e. falling upon the knees, then gradually inclining the body, until the forehead touched the ground) was common as an expression of profound reverence and humility before a superior or a benefactor. It was practiced in the worship of Yahweh (Genesis 17:3 Numbers 16:45 Matthew 26:39, Jesus in Gethsemane; Revelation 1:17), The highest form of adoration is that which is directed immediately to God himself, his kingly attributes and spiritual excellencies being so apprehended by the soul that it is filled with rapture and praise, and is moved to do Him reverence. A classical instance is the vision that initiated Isaiah into the prophetic office, when he was so possessed with the sovereignty and sublimity of God that he was filled with wonder and self-abasement (Isaiah 6:1-5). In the Old Testament, the literature of adoration reaches its high-water mark in the Psalms (compare especially the group Psalms 95-100), where the ineffable majesty, power and Holiness of God are set forth in lofty strains. In the New Testament, adoration of the Deity finds its most rapturous expression in Revelations, where the vision of God calls forth a chorus of praise addressed to the thrice-Holy God.* End of quotation.

Confession that comes through adoration ultimately brings forgiveness due to the fact that God's judgment is on sin. A time is coming when we will all give thanks for the finished work of Jesus Christ! To reiterate what has been stated before, God is magnified and glorified throughout all of His creation as He demonstrates complete love, forgiveness, and mercy through His righteous judgments to each of us that come to Him by faith and verbal confession.

Every satanic power and created demonic principality including God's Holy angelic realm peer into the spiritual struggles of humanity to witness God's dealings with each individual. These satanic powers and demonic principalities including God's angelic realm will witness God's dealings with humanity with either contempt and pure hatred or adoration and pure joy!

Jesus came to save that which is lost! He said; *"Father forgive them, for they know not what they do!"* Yes, God is very much alive, and He is very much in perfect control of every detail, and of every situation, knowing full well every persons circumstance. God has counted the unfathomable cost of all the suffering in this world and has placed all of it upon the shoulders of His perfect, sinless Son Jesus Christ! Not only did He do this, but He poured out His wrath upon His Son, and forsook Him! He did this, so that we would not be forsaken by God and destroyed by the very wrath we deserve. Merriam-Webster's Dictionary defines wrath as; *1) Strong vengeful anger or indignation, 2) retributory punishment for an offense or a crime: divine chastisement.*

Luke, a Gentile physician and associate of Paul had this to say in Acts 3:17-21; *Friends, I realize that what you did to Jesus was done in ignorance; and the same can be said of your leaders. But God was fulfilling what all the prophets had declared about the Messiah beforehand–that He must suffer all these things. Now turn from your sins and turn to God, so you can be cleansed of your sins. Then wonderful times of refreshment will come from the presence of the Lord, and He will send Jesus your Messiah to you again. For He must remain in Heaven until the time for the final restoration of all things, as God promised long ago through His prophets* NLT.

With a new understanding of what it means to be lowered into the realm of carnality thus resulting in a depraved nature, it should be evident to each person reading this book, just how easily we can get ourselves into trouble when operating in the realm of carnality. God will never leave us completely alone in that realm because it is there that we all will find Him. I thank God that His judgments are filled with undeserved mercy. That's His justice over sin! In chapter 28, we will examine numerous Scripture passages confirming God's heart for all.

24

Is Salvation For The Wicked Fair?

If we are to ask this question from a human perspective, more than likely our natural inclination would be to demand of God His condemnation of the wicked with an everlasting punishment. Without Godly wisdom and revelation on this subject, we cannot even begin to understand God's ways concerning the wicked. Scripture declares that, *"God's ways are past finding out"* and that, *"All things are possible with God."* Judgmental self righteous pride prevents us from understanding God's loving mercy that He may have towards others. It's easy to feel this way when we convince ourselves that God is not dealing with the wicked as we insist He should.

Depravity working in un-regenerated lives cause those individuals to repeat ungodly acts over and over again, and yet they seek the world's mercy and forgiveness. Those that are "born again" of the Spirit can act just as ungodly, and yet find ways to seek God's mercy and forgiveness over and over again as well. We are told by Jesus that if we so much as even hate another person in our heart regardless of whom we are–His Father sees that hatred as equal to murder. Because God is extremely interested in the development of our character, any impure motive of our heart will be effectively dealt with as we suffer through the effects of sinful activity operating within our personal lives. This is why we are called to leave our evil ways, and walk in the ways of the righteousness of Jesus Christ.

"Love your enemies! Do good to them! Lend to them! And don't be concerned that they might not repay. Then your reward from Heaven will be very great, and you will truly be acting as children of the Most High, for He is kind to the unthankful and to those who are wicked Luke 6:35 NLT.

25

The Eleventh Hour

In the 20th chapter of Matthew, Jesus speaks of the "Eleventh Hour" in the telling of the "Parable of The Vineyard." Let's have a look at this parable in context.

"For the kingdom of Heaven is like a land owner who went out early in the morning to hire laborers for his vineyard. Now when he had agreed with the laborers for a denarius a day, he sent them into his vineyard. And he went out about the third hour and saw others standing idle in the marketplace, and said to them, "You also go into the vineyard, and whatever is right I will give you." So they went. Again he went out about the sixth and the ninth hour, and did likewise, and about the eleventh hour he went out and found others standing idle, and said to them, "Why have you been standing here idle all day? They said to him, "Because no one hired us." He said to them, "You also go into the vineyard, and whatever is right, you will receive." So when evening had come, the owner of the vineyard said to his steward, "Call the laborers and give them their wages, beginning with the last to the first." And when those came who were hired about the eleventh hour, they each received a denarius. But when the first came, they supposed that they would receive more; and they likewise received each a denarius. And when they had received it, they complained against the landowner saying, "These last men have worked only one hour, and you made them equal to us

who have borne the burden and the heat of the day." But he answered one of them and said, "Friend, I am doing you no wrong. Did you not agree with me for a denarius? Take what is yours and go your way, I wish to give to this last man the same as you. Is it not lawful for me to do what I wish with my own things? Or is your eye (understanding) evil because I am good? So the last will be first, and the first last. For many are called, but few chosen."

Much can be gleaned from this parable. I wish however, to emphasis the "Eleventh Hour." The eleventh hour is the central focus of this biblical teaching. The eleventh hour according to the Wikipedia Encyclopedia is; *"A figure of speech referring to the last moments before a deadline, or meant to imply that a decisive or "Final" moment is near."*

In the above Scripture passage, those that were found to be standing idle, were hired about the eleventh hour. I believe the implications of this parable demonstrates that within the final moments of God's judgments, His justice is served through mercy in the "Eleventh Hour." Convicts on death row at times receive a stay of execution on a technicality in the "Eleventh Hour." Why would our loving God be any different?

26

The Sheep And Goats

We have come to the place in our journey when we will examine the parable of the separation of the "Sheep And Goats," and the parable of "The Ten Virgins." To begin with, let us look at a Scripture passage found in Mathew 25:31–46.

"When the Son of Man comes in His Glory, and all the Holy angels with Him, then He will sit on the throne of His glory. All nations will be gathered before Him, and He will separate them one from another, as a shepherd divides his sheep from the goats. And He will set the sheep on His right hand, but the goats on the left. Then the King will say to those on His right hand, "Come, you blessed of my Father, inherit the kingdom prepared for you from the foundation of the world; for I was hungry and you gave Me food; I was thirsty and you gave me drink; I was a stranger and you took Me in; I was naked and you clothed Me; I was in prison and you came to Me." Then the righteous will answer Him saying, "Lord, when did we see You hungry and feed You, of thirsty and give You drink? When did we see You a stranger and take You in, or naked and clothe You? Or when did we see You sick, or in prison, and come to You?" And the King will answer and say to them, "Assuredly, I say to you, inasmuch as you did it to one of the least of these My brethren, you did it to Me." Then He will say to those on the left hand, "Depart from Me, you cursed,

into everlasting fire prepared for the Devil and his angels; for I was hungry and you gave Me no food; I was thirsty and you gave Me no drink; I was a stranger and you did not take Me in, naked and you did not clothe Me, sick and in prison and you did not visit Me." Then they also will answer Him, saying, "Lord, when did we see You hungry or thirsty or a stranger or naked or sick or in prison, and did not minister to You?" Then He will answer them saying, "Assuredly, I say to you, inasmuch as you did not do it to one of the least of these, you did not do it to Me." And these will go away into everlasting punishment, but the righteous into eternal life."

Late one night the above mentioned passage was being discussed on–line with a group of several individuals. One of those individuals was a fellow by the name of Jonathan Mitchell. This is what he had to say about the "Sheep and the Goats." **I quote;** *"I do not think that this passage in Matthew refers to mankind in a general kind of way at all, but to God's chosen people–the Jews. The judgment is for them, in this passage. Note that both the sheep and the goats were a part of His herd, and both were clean animals which were used in Israel's sacrifices (e.g., during Passover–a lamb; during Tabernacles, "Atonement" was via goats). This passage demonstrates that God does, from time to time (note: this was not some final separation of the Shepherd's herds, but was for a specific purpose), makes separations (the root meaning of "judge") for various stages of His purposes in His people. Here, we see that some are ready to enjoy the inheritance of the kingdom. Why? They were mature sheep (not lambs needing milk) and they demonstrated a nature of love and caring; serving–even thoughtlessly. When had they done this to Him? The environment was kingdom life, for they did these things to His brothers. They were mature, and they were to go their way, following this review by the Shepherd, and continue in eonian life of the kingdom. Not so, the kids (they were not mature goats, but, literally, "kids"). They had expressed no such maturity of love in their lives, and were probably oblivious to the needs of others. Thus,* *their next phase amidst His brothers was an indefinite period of "Pruning," or "Lopping Off" on their non-fruit-bearing branches (e.g.,* John 15:2, 6-8).

I believe that this parable first applied to those of first-century Israel: some were to enter into the kingdom; (those branches of the olive tree which were not broken out Romans 11:17) *the kids were the branches which were broken out of the olive tree, to be grafted back in at a later time* Romans 11:23. *They were to experience a period of His purifying fire (also called "Pruning" in* Matthew 25:46). *What happened to them will happen to us, as well. Thus does He yet deal with His people. For Love would bring all into His image and have them doing as did the sheep in our parable. I see this as on-going in each of our lives, as He lovingly brings correction to our walk, and pruning that we would bear even more fruit. We are His vineyard, His orchard. Both are seasonally pruned."* **End of quotation.**

27

The Ten Virgins

Not all of God's children will be carriers of His glory. The parable of "The Ten Virgins," brings together much needed insight concerning this fact in the clearest way possible. Let us begin with a passage of Scripture as found in Matthew 25:1–13.

"Then the kingdom of Heaven shall be likened to ten virgins who took their lamps and went out to meet the bridegroom. Now five of them were wise, and five were foolish. Those who were foolish took their lamps and took no oil with them. But the wise took oil in their vessels with their lamps. But while the bridegroom was delayed, they all slumbered and slept. And at midnight a cry was heard; "Behold, the bridegroom is coming; go out to meet him!" Then all those virgins arose and trimmed their lamps. And the foolish said to the wise, "Give us some of your oil, for our lamps are going out." But the wise answered saying, "No, lest there should not be enough for us and you; but go rather to those who sell, and buy for yourselves." And while they went to buy, the bridegroom came, and those who were ready went in with him to the wedding; and the door was shut. Afterward the other virgins came also, saying, "Lord, Lord, open to us!" But he answered and said, "Assuredly, I say to you, I do not know you." Watch therefore, for you know neither the day nor the hour in which the Son of Man is coming."

Some definitions of the word virgin found in Webster's Dictionary are as follows; 1) mother of Jesus; 2) unmarried women devoted to her religion; 3) a person who has not had sexual intercourse; 4) free from stain; 5) pure; 6) spotless; 7) chaste; 8) modest; 9) fresh; 10) unspoiled; and 11) not altered by human activity.

These definitions are not meant to emphasize sexual purity but rather, to give the idea that the "Ten Virgins" in this parable represent all of humanity from God's perspective as He sees them–once cleansed by the blood of Jesus Christ, even though this cleansing may not be fully realized by the "five foolish virgins." In other words, wise and foolish choices can still be made in the carnality of our flesh even while being covered by the blood of Jesus Christ! It is possible to be a goat (foolish virgin) or a sheep (wise virgin) and be separated from each other and from Christ for seasons of time until all come into maturity!

Notice that the above mentioned Scripture passage starts off by saying; *"Then the kingdom of Heaven shall be likened to ten virgins."* Even though five of the virgins are foolish, none the less, they are still virgin. This is a very important point to keep in mind, even with the groom saying in verse 12; *"Assuredly, I say to you, I do not know you."* The five foolish virgins are still part of God's kingdom! They are still covered by the blood of Jesus, otherwise they would not be deemed "virgin." When we come to Christ by faith through personal repentance, we are transformed through new birth and deemed "virgin" in the sight of God by the shed blood of Jesus.

I believe that the taking away of rewards has something to do with the foolish virgins not having a sufficient supply of oil in their lamps, thus missing out on the "Marriage Super Of The Lamb, "by being cast out for not being ready, and on time!They are still the Lord's, but due to the fact that they had a superficial relationship with Him, Jesus could honestly say to them, that He did not know them. Perhaps the best way to summarize the significance of what I'm trying to say is that anyone can call upon the name of the Lord and know of Him, but the most important question is, have you made Him Lord of your life?

Is it possible that the reward for the laying of treasure up in Heaven becomes the key that opens God's Kingdom to us, through the development of a deep and intimate relationship with our Savior by conscious choice? I believe that the symbolism of the oil as found in the parable of the "Ten Virgins" is to a large extent, an indication of the depth of our relationship with Jesus! The foolish virgins had a superficial supply of oil that ran out. Out of desperation they were trying to acquire some oil for their lamps from the wise virgins. How can anyone be expected to give to someone else a measure of oil that cannot be bought, but in fact can only be acquired through the development of personal relationships? I do believe however, that eventually God's grace and mercy will come to all those who have no oil in there lamps, as He Himself pours in the oil. This is just like the Father that I have come to know would do! He will not chastise the outcast, the un-loveable, the underdog, or the wicked forever.

28

Reconciliation Scriptures (NKJV)

In your seed __all__ the nations of the earth shall be blessed, because you have obeyed My voice. Genesis 22:18.

And I will make your descendants multiply as the stars of Heaven; I will give to your descendants all these lands; and in your seed __all__ the nations of the earth shall be blessed. Genesis 26:4.

Also your descendants shall be as the dust of the earth; you shall be spread abroad to the west and the east, to the north and the south; and in you and your seed __all__ the families of the earth shall be blessed. Genesis 28:14.

Ask of Me, and I will give You the __nations for Your inheri-__ __tance, and the __ends of the earth for Your possession__. Psalm 2:8.

__All__ the ends of the world shall remember and turn to the Lord, and __all__ the families of the nations shall worship before you. For the kingdom is the Lord's and He rules over the nations. __All__ the prosperous of the earth shall eat and wor-ship; __all those who go down to the dust shall bow before Him,__ __even he who cannot keep himself alive__. Psalm 22:27-29.

O You who hear prayer, to You __all__ flesh (men) will come. Iniquities prevail against me; __as for our transgressions, You__ __will provide atonement for them__. Psalm 65:2, 3.

Yes, __all__ Kings shall fall down before Him; all nations shall

serve Him. *His name shall endure forever; His name shall continue as long as the sun. And men shall be blessed in Him; <u>all</u>
nations shall call Him blessed.* Psalm 72:11, 17.

*<u>All</u> nations whom You have made shall come and wor-
ship before You, O Lord, and shall glorify Your name. For You
are great, and do wondrous things; You alone are God.* Psalm
86:9, 10.

*O give thanks to the Lord, for He is good! For His <u>mercy
endures forever.</u>* Psalm 107:1.

*The Lord is good to <u>all</u>, and His tender mercies are over <u>all</u>
His works.* Psalm 145:9.

*My mouth shall speak the praise of the Lord, and <u>all</u> flesh
shall bless His Holy name forever and ever.* Psalm 145:21.

*"Come now, and <u>let us reason together</u>," says the Lord,
"<u>Though your sins are like scarlet, they shall be as white
as snow; though they are red like crimson, they shall be as
wool.</u>"* Isaiah 1:18.

*They shall not hurt nor destroy in <u>all</u> My Holy mountain,
<u>for the earth shall be full of the knowledge of the Lord as the
waters cover the sea.</u>* Isaiah 11:9.

*And in this mountain the Lord of hosts will make for <u>all</u>
people a feast of choice pieces, a feast of wines on the lees, of
fat things full of marrow, of well-refined wines on the lees.
And He will destroy on this mountain the surface of the covering cast over <u>all</u> people, and the veil that is spread over <u>all</u>
nations. He will swallow up death forever, and the Lord God
will wipe away tears from <u>all</u> faces; the rebuke of His people
He will take away from <u>all</u> the earth; for the Lord has spoken.*
Isaiah 25:6-8.

*With my soul I have desired You in the night, yes, by my
spirit within me I will seek You early; <u>for when Your judgments are in the earth, the inhabitants of the world will learn
righteousness.</u>* Isaiah 26:9.

*The Glory of the Lord shall be revealed, and <u>all</u> flesh shall
see it together; for the mouth of the Lord has spoken.* Isaiah
40: 5.

"You have bought Me no sweet cane with money, nor

have you satisfied Me with the fat of your sacrifices; but you have burdened Me with your sins, you have wearied Me with Your iniquities. I, even I, am He who blots out your transgressions for My own sake; and I will not remember your sins." Isaiah 43:24, 25.

Declaring the end from the beginning, and from ancient times things that are yet done, saying, "My counsel shall stand, and I will do all My pleasure." Isaiah 46:10.

Surely He has borne our griefs and carried our sorrows; yet we esteemed Him stricken, smitten by God, and afflicted. But He was wounded for our transgressions, He was bruised for our iniquities; the chastisement for our peace was upon Him, and by His stripes we are healed. All we like sheep have gone astray; we have turned, every one, to his own way; and the Lord has laid on Him the iniquity of us all. Isaiah 53:4-6.

So shall My word be that goes forth from My mouth; it shall not return to Me void, but it shall accomplish what I please, and it shall prosper in the thing for which I send it. Isaiah 55:11.

For I will not contend for ever, nor will I always be angry; for the spirit would fail before Me, and the souls which I have made. Isaiah 57:16.

Arise, shine; for your light has come! And the glory of the Lord is risen upon you. For behold, the darkness shall cover the earth, and deep darkness the people; but the Lord will arise over you, and His glory will be seen upon you. The Gentiles shall come to your light, and kings to the brightness of your rising. Isaiah 60:1-3.

"And it shall come to pass that from one New Moon to another, and from one Sabbath to another, all flesh (mankind) shall come to worship before Me," says the Lord. Isaiah 66:23.

"Behold, the days are coming, says the Lord, when I will make a new covenant with the house of Israel and with the house of Judah–not according to the covenant that I made with their fathers in the day that I took them by the hand to lead them out of the land of Egypt, My covenant which they broke, though I was a husband to them says the Lord.

But this is the covenant that I will make with the house of Israel after those days, says the lord; I will put My law in their minds, and write it on their hearts; and I will be their God, and they shall be My people. No more shall every man teach his neighbor, and every man his brother, saying, know the Lord, for they all shall know Me, from the least of them to the greatest of them, says the Lord. For I will forgive their iniquity, and their sin I will remember no more." Jeremiah 31; 31-34.

"Now I, Nebuchadnezzar, praise and extol and honor the King of Heaven, all of whose works are truth, and His ways justice. And those who walk in pride He is able to put down." Daniel 4:37.

Then to Him was given dominion and glory and a Kingdom, that all peoples, nations, and languages should serve Him. His dominion is an everlasting dominion, which shall not pass away, and His Kingdom is the one which shall not destroyed. Daniel 7:14.

Who is a God like You, pardoning iniquity and passing over the transgression of the remnant of His heritage? He does not retain His anger forever, because He delights in mercy. He will again have compassion on us, and will subdue our iniquities. You will cast all our sins into the depths of the sea. Micah 7:18-19.

For the earth will be filled with the knowledge of the glory of the Lord, as the waters cover the sea. Habakkuk 2:14.

For then I will restore to the peoples a pure language, that they all may call on the name of the Lord, to serve Him with one accord. Zephaniah 3:9.

"For from the rising of the sun, even to its going down, My name shall be great among the Gentiles; in every place incense shall be offered to My name, and a pure offering; for My name shall be great among the nations," says the Lord of hosts.* Malachi 1:11.

For the Lord will not cast off forever. Though He causes grief, yet He will show compassion according to the multitude *of <u>His mercies</u>.* Lamentations 3:31, 32.

Then the angel said to them, "Do not be afraid, for behold, I bring you good tidings of great joy which will be to <u>all</u> people. For there is born to you this day in the city of David a Savior, who is Christ the Lord." Luke 2:10, 11.

And <u>all flesh</u> shall see the salvation of God. Luke 3:6.

That was the true light which gives light to <u>every man</u> coming into the world. John 1:9.

The next day John saw Jesus coming toward Him, and said, "<u>Behold! The Lamb Of God who takes away the sin of the world!</u>" John 1:29.

For God did not send His Son into the world to condemn the world, <u>but to save the world through Him</u>. John 3:17

Then they said to the woman, "Now we believe, not because of what you said, for we ourselves have heard Him and we know that this is indeed the Christ, <u>the Savior of the world</u>." John 4:42.

"And I, if I am lifted up from the earth, will draw <u>all</u> peoples to Myself." **John 12:32.**

And if any one hears My words and does not believe, I do not judge "him; for <u>I did not come to judge the world but to save the world</u>." John 12:47.

... and that He may send Jesus Christ, who was preached to you before, whom Heaven must receive <u>until the times of restoration of all things</u>, which God has spoken by the mouth of all His holy prophets since the world began. Acts 3:20, 21.

Therefore, as through one man's offence judgment came to <u>all</u> men, resulting in condemnation, even so through one Man's righteous act the free gift came to <u>all</u> men, resulting in justification of life. Romans 5:18.

For earnest expectation of the creation eagerly waits for the revealing of the sons of God. For the creation was subjected to futility, not willingly, but because of Him who subjected it in hope; <u>because the creation itself also will be delivered from bondage of corruption into the glorious liberty of the children of God</u>. For we know that the whole creation groans and labors with birth pangs together until now.

Romans 8:19-22.

For if their being cast away is <u>*the reconciling of the*</u> <u>*world, what will their acceptance be but life from the dead?*</u> Romans 11:15.

And so <u>*all*</u> *Israel will be saved, as it is written: the deliverer will come out of Zion, and He will turn away ungodliness from Jacob;* <u>*for this is my covenant with them, when I*</u> <u>*take away their sins.*</u> Romans 11:26, 27.

For God has committed them <u>*all*</u> *to disobedience, that He might have mercy on* <u>*all.*</u> *Oh, the depth of the riches both of the wisdom and knowledge of God! How unsearchable are His judgments and His ways past finding out!* Romans 11:32, 33.

For of Him and through Him and to Him are <u>*all*</u> *things, to whom be the glory forever. Amen.* Romans 11:36.

<u>*Love does no harm to a neighbor, therefore love is the ful-*</u><u>*fillment of the law.*</u> *And do this, knowing the time, that* <u>*now*</u> <u>*it is high time to awake out of sleep; for now our salvation is*</u> <u>*nearer than when we first believed.*</u> Romans 13:10, 11.

For no other foundation can anyone lay than that which is laid, which is Jesus Christ. Now if <u>*anyone*</u> *builds on this foundation with gold, silver, precious stones, wood, hay, straw, each one's work will declare it, because it will be revealed by fire; and the fire will test each one's work, of what sort it is. If anyone's work which he has built on it endures, he will receive a reward. If anyone's work is burned,* <u>*he will*</u> <u>*suffer loss; but he himself will be saved, yet so as through fire.*</u> 1Corinthians 3:11-15.

For as in Adam <u>*all*</u> *die, even so in Christ* <u>*all*</u> *shall be made alive.* 1 Corinthians 15:22.

The <u>*last enemy*</u> *that will be* <u>*destroyed*</u> *is* <u>*death.*</u> 1 Corinthians 15:26.

Now <u>*all*</u> *things are of God, who has* <u>*reconciled us*</u> *to Himself through Jesus Christ, and has given us* <u>*the ministry of*</u> <u>*reconciliation,*</u> *that is that God was in Christ* <u>*reconciling the*</u> <u>*world to Himself, not imputing their trespasses to them,*</u> *and has committed to us the word of* <u>*reconciliation.*</u> *Now then,* *we are ambassadors for Christ, as though God were pleading through us: we implore you on Christ's behalf, <u>be reconciled to God</u>.* 2 Corinthians 5:18-20.

Therefore God also has highly exalted Him and given Him the name which is above every name, that at the name of Jesus <u>every knee should bow , of those in heaven , and of those on earth , and of those under the earth, and that every tongue should confess that Jesus Christ is Lord , to the glory of God the Father</u>. Philippians 2:9-11.

<u>He has delivered us from the power of darkness and con- veyed us into the kingdom of the Son of His love</u>, in whom we have <u>redemption</u> through His blood, the forgiveness of sins. He is the image of the invisible God, the firstborn over <u>all</u> cre- ation. For by Him <u>all</u> things were created that are in Heaven and that are on earth, visible and invisible, whether thrones or dominions or principalities or powers. <u>All</u> things were cre- ated through Him and for Him. And He is before <u>all</u> things, and in Him <u>all</u> things consist. Colossians 1:13-17.

... and by Him to <u>reconcile all things to Himself</u> , by Him, whether things on earth or things in Heaven, having made peace through the blood of His cross. Colossians 1:20.

This is a faithful saying and worthy of <u>all acceptance</u>, that <u>Christ Jesus came into the world to save sinners</u>, of whom I am chief. 1 Timothy 1:15.

For this is good and acceptable in the sight of God our Savior, who desires <u>all</u> men to be saved and come into the knowledge of the truth. For there is one God and one Mediator between God and men, the Man Jesus Christ, who gave Himself a ransom for <u>all</u>, to be testified in due time. 1 Timothy 2:-3-6.

This is a faithful saying and worthy of all acceptance. For to this end we both labor and suffer reproach, because we trust in the living God, who is <u>the Savior of all men espe- cially of those who believe.</u> These things command and teach. 1 Timothy 4:9-11.

For the grace of God that brings salvation has appeared to <u>all</u> men. Titus 2:11.

But we see Jesus, who was made a little lower than the

angels, for the suffering of death crowned with glory and honor, that He, by the grace of God, might taste death for <u>everyone</u>. Hebrews 2:9.

None of them shall teach his neighbor, and none his brother, saying, "Know the Lord, <u>for all shall know me, from the least of them to the greatest of them. For I will be merciful to their unrighteousness, and their sins and their lawless deeds I will remember no more</u>." Hebrews 8:11, 12.

For Christ also suffered <u>once</u> for sins, the just for the unjust , that He might bring us to God, being put to death in the flesh but made alive in the Spirit, by whom also <u>He went and preached to the spirits in prison</u>, who formerly were disobedient, when once the Devine long suffering waited in the days of Noah, while the ark was being prepared, in which a few that is, eight souls, were saved through water. 1 Peter 3:18-20.

<u>For this reason the gospel was preached also to those who are dead</u>, that they might be judged according to men in the flesh, <u>but live according to God in the spirit</u>. 1 Peter 4: 6.

The Lord is not slack concerning His promise, as some count slackness, but is long suffering toward us, not willing that <u>any</u> should perish but that <u>all</u> should come to repentance. 2 Peter 3:9.

And He Himself is the propitiation (atoning sacrifice) for our sins, and not for ours only <u>but also for the whole world</u>. 1 John 2:2.

And we have seen and testify that the Father has sent the Son as <u>Savior of the world</u>. 1 John 4:14.

And <u>every creature</u> which is in Heaven and on the earth and under the earth and such as are in the sea, and <u>all</u> that are in them, I heard saying: <u>Blessing and honor and glory and power be to Him who sits on the throne and to the Lamb, forever and ever</u>! Revelation 5:13.

<u>Who shall not fear You</u>, O Lord, and <u>glorify your name</u>? For You alone are Holy. For <u>all</u> nations shall come and worship before You, for Your judgments have been manifested. Revelation 15:4.

And I heard a loud voice in Heaven saying, "<u>Behold, the</u>

tabernacle is with men, and He will dwell with them, and they shall be His people. God Himself will be with them and be their God. And God will wipe away every tear from their eyes; there shall be no more death, nor sorrow, nor crying. There shall be no more pain, for the former things have passed away." Then He who sat on the throne said, "Behold, I make all things new." And He said to me, "Write, for these words are true and faithful." Revelation 21:3-5.

29

The Origins of Evil

What are the origins of evil? I have asked God this very question many times. Some of you may be surprised or even shocked with what Scripture actually reveals about the origins of evil.

I personally have been taught to believe certain things concerning evil and how to battle it in my life, but have not received any substantial teaching or instruction on its ultimate purpose–until recently.

Only the pure "Light" of God can cast out and shatter darkness! If you think about that for a moment, it's not difficult to see that the darkness of evil becomes the contrast created by God for the manifestation of His "Light" to be seen with physical eyes, but more importantly understood through spiritual eyes. With this insight, let us explore the subject of evil, starting with a commentary written by an anonymous author as gleaned from the public domain. The quoted article (used with permission) is titled; "Misrepresenting The Word Of God."

I quote, *"Far too many theologians misrepresent the Word of God, and therefore pervert it to suit their unscriptural biases. I have heard of theologians who graduated from seminary and still did not know that God says in* Isaiah 45:7; *I form the light and create darkness, I make peace and create evil. I, the Lord do all these things.* NKJV. *And most who have read it, don't believe it.*

Evil has no moral bias. God does not sin when He uses evil for His good purposes. Men sin when they do evil to other men. Evil (Heb. Ha' = to smash) is only a "sin" when it is used wrongly. God uses evil for good. The glorious culmination of God's plan will justify His use of evil a trillion times to the power of infinity! Notice how often He uses evil in the Scriptures.

*Authors note: I have chosen certain Bible translations for each of the following Scripture passages as indicated after each passage that best emphasize and support the points being made by the writer of this article. I have also looked up and compared each of the listed passages with the following Bible translations; NKJV, Contemporary English Version, ESV, Good News Translation, NAS, NIV, NLT, New Life Bible, and Greens Literal Translation and have found them all to be very close in resemblance and contextual meaning.

Out of the mouth of the most High proceedeth not evil and good? Lamentations 3:38, KJV.

And I gave my heart to seek and to investigate by wisdom concerning all which is done under the heavens. It is an evil task God has given to the sons of men, to be afflicted by it. Ecclesiastes 1:13, Green's Literal Translation.

Thus saith the Lord, Behold, I will raise up evil against thee out of thine own house, and I will take thy wives before thine eyes, and give them unto thy neighbour, and he shall lie with thy wives in the sight of this sun. 2 Samuel 12:11, KJV.

Thou wilt say then unto me, why doth He yet find fault? For who hath resisted His will? Nay but, O man, who art thou that repliest against God? Shall the thing formed say to Him that formed it, why hast thou made me thus? Hath not the potter power over the clay, of the same lump to make one vessel unto honour, and another unto dishonour? Romans 9:19-21 KJV.

Behold, I have created the smith who blows the coal in the fire, and who brings out a weapon for His work; and I have created the waster to destroy. Isaiah 54:16, Green's Literal

Translation.

The Lord hath made all things for Himself: yea, even the wicked for the day of evil. Proverbs 16:4, KJV.

Lift up a banner toward Zion. Flee for safety and do not wait. For I will bring evil from the north and a great ruin. Jeremiah 4:6, Green's Literal Translation.

Hear O earth. Behold, I will bring evil upon this people, even the fruit of their thoughts, because they have not hearkened unto My words, nor to My law, but rejected it. Jeremiah 6:19, KJV.

The Lord said to him, "In what way?" So he said, "I will go out and be a lying spirit in the mouth of all his prophets." And the Lord said, "You shall persuade him, and also prevail. Go out and do so." 1 Kings 22:22 NKJV.

He (God) turned their heart to hate His people... Psalms 105:25, NKJV.

...Thus saith the Lord; "Behold, I frame evil against you, and devise a device against you..." Jeremiah 18:11, KJV.

For God has committed them all to disobedience, that He might have mercy on all. Romans 11:32, NKJV.

O Lord, why have You made us stray from Your ways, and hardened our heart from Your fear? Isaiah 63:17, NKJV.

...so shall the Lord bring upon you all evil things, until He have destroyed you from off this good land... Joshua 23:15, KJV.

...shall there be evil in a city, and the Lord hath not done it? Amos 3:6, KJV.

And you have forgotten the exhortation which speaks to you as to sons: "My son, do not despise the chastening of the Lord, nor be discouraged when you are rebuked by Him ..." Hebrews 12:5, NKJV.

By His Spirit He hath garnished the heavens; His hand hath formed the crooked serpent. Job 26:13, KJV.

So the great dragon was cast out, that serpent of old, called the Devil and Satan... Revelation 12:9, NKJV.

He who sins is of the devil, for the devil has sinned from the beginning. 1 John 3:8, NKJV.

... "What? shall we receive good at the hand of God, and shall we not receive evil?" In all this did not Job sin with his lips. Job 2:10 also see 42:7, KJV.

Thus says the Lord of hosts: "...Now go and attack Amalek, and utterly destroy all that they have, and do not spare them. But kill both man and woman, infant and nursing child..." 1 Samuel 15:2, 3, NKJV.

... God will send them strong delusion, that they should believe the lie. 2 Thessalonians 2:11, 12, NKJV.

Scripture proves that God not only created evil, but that He Himself is responsible for it. Maybe these aren't Sunday School verses, but they are Scripture. These are strong verses. At times it is hard to emotionally deal with the evils of this world. But I thank God that He, and not Satan or man controls evil. It is important to understand that God puts limitations on evil. He doesn't use it indiscriminately. Jeremiah 18:11 says; *... Thus saith the Lord; Behold, I frame evil against you, and devise a device against you: return ye now everyone from his evil way, and make your ways and your doings good.* KJV. *This verse alone shows the boundaries and limitations that God Himself puts on evil.*

It is paramount that we clearly understand one thing in God's creation and use of evil, lest my detractors accuse me of saying that God is evil. James 1:13 *says; Let no one say when he is tempted, "I am tempted by God," for God cannot be tempted by evil, nor does He Himself tempt anyone.*

God has so constituted man to be (naturally) spiritually weak. For the disposition (Greek phronema, results of one's inclinations, of the flesh), is death, yet the disposition of the spirit is life and peace, because the disposition of the flesh is enmity (the bitter feeling that enemies have; hatred) with God, for it is not subject to the law of God, for neither is it able Romans 8:7 *Without God, His Spirit and His love, this is the disposition of all flesh (mankind, humanity).*

The Scriptures say that; All things are of God... 2 Corinthians 5:18. *Yet we just read that God ... is trying no one. That is, God Himself is not trying or testing us to see how well we fare. He already knows the verdict. He already knows, that we don't "fare" well at all. God knows all. 1 John 3:20.*

The reason God doesn't Himself try anyone is because He doesn't need to try anyone for His benefit, He already knows all. Notice Webster's Dictionary: trial, 1. the act of hearing a case in a law court to decide whether the claim or charge is true. Surely, no one is so audacious as to think God needs evidence in a trial to determine the truth. God sends the trials, but God does not do the trying. He already knows the outcome but man doesn't. Man desperately needs trials to prove to himself (not to God) that he is a failure and needs a Savior. The trials are for our benefit, for our learning, not for God's benefit and God's learning. God knows all.

We can accomplish no good of ourselves. What we are to learn is contained in the next passage; Do not be deceived (but of course, most people are deceived), my beloved brethren. Every good gift and every perfect gift is from above, and comes down from the Father of lights. James 1:16. That is the lesson we, not God, are to learn. Our trials are a great aid in understanding God's goodness.

Again, consider Joseph and his brothers. Joseph told his brothers; But now, do not therefore be grieved nor angry with yourselves because you sold me here... Genesis 45:5. What? Don't be grieved, or angry with yourselves, for committing such atrocious sins, crimes, and evils? This was certainly a severe trial on Joseph and his brothers. God brought it all about, not so He could see how they would handle this trial. God already knew that. That's why God, Himself, tries no one. ...for God sent me before you to preserve life (same verse). Not so that God would learn something He didn't already know. How silly. It was all of God, and the end more than justified the means. Why do men doubt God's ability to bring about good from evil, and to save mankind in the only way they could ever really appreciate God's love and goodness? Even the greatest of evils, death, will be swallowed up in victory. 1 Corinthians 15:54.

For as in Adam all die, even so in Christ all shall be

made alive. 1 Corinthians 15:22. *What was God's purpose in bringing this severe trial on Joseph and his brothers? ...And God sent me before you to preserve a posterity for you in the earth, and to save your lives by a great deliverance. So now it was not you who sent me here, but God; and He has made me a father to Pharaoh, and lord of all his house, and a ruler throughout all the land of Egypt.* Genesis 45:7, 8.

God's plan is all about life. God creates life. God chastises us in life. God makes life miserable at times. We are often weak and diseased in life. Even still, we love our own lives. But ultimately, God takes away our lives. Our parents die, our friends and relatives die. We know for certain that we, ourselves, will die. Without faith, it is a frightening expectation. But, we will all be overwhelmed with joy when God finally gives back our lives with immortality, never to suffer, sorrow, or hurt again. We simply need to trust God. We'll all be so glad we took the journey when we arrive at the journey's end.

So no, God is not evil, but God has determined and declared that we all must experience a certain amount of evil in this life. Nonetheless, God is still going to scourge every son whom He receives. Let's have a look at Hebrews 12:5, 6. *And you have forgotten the exhortation which speaks to you as to sons: "My son, do not despise the chastening of the Lord, nor be discouraged when you are rebuked by Him; for whom the Lord loves He chastens, and scourges (intensely prick, whip or flog, cause great pain or suffering) every son whom He receives.*

Was Paul unacquainted with evil? I think not. In 2 Corinthians 11:23 – 27 *he writes: ... in labors more abundant, in stripes above measure, in prisons more frequently, in deaths often. From the Jews five times I received forty stripes minus one. Three times I was beaten with rods; once I was stoned; three times I was shipwrecked; a night and a day I have been in the deep; in journeys often, in perils of waters, in perils of robbers, in perils of my own countrymen, in perils of the Gentiles, in perils in the city, in perils in the wilderness, in perils in the sea, in perils among false brethren; in weariness and toil, in sleeplessness often, in hunger and thirst, in fastings often, in cold and nakedness–besides the other things, what comes upon me daily–my deep concern for all the churches. This is not to mention all the daily problems of the churches. And Paul was well aware that it was God who brought all these evils upon him, even though God may have used intermediaries. Even so Paul's ministry was beyond reproach. See also* 2 Corinthians 12:7, Acts 9:16 *and* 2 Timothy 2:9.

Even if one denies the truth of these Scriptures, one still has to deal with providence, Recently fifteen people died in a Colorado school. That's tragic. A week later fifty people died from tornadoes. That too was tragic. Recently, over ten thousand souls died in an earthquake in Turkey. Next, thousands perished in an earthquake in Taiwan, with still more thousands buried alive. Not that long ago, six hundred thousand perished in a typhoon in Bangladesh and the disease that followed may have raised the toll to one million. One may suppose God's eyes were closed during the Colorado school shooting. But who would deny that God controls the forces of nature and the weather? Look at what we call nature. Nature is filled with evil. In nature almost every living creature eats another living creature for lunch. Lions eat deer. Foxes eat rabbits. Big fish eat little fish. All creatures engage in a life-time vigil for their own preservation.

The sun gives warmth and life, but also causes skin cancer. The air gives life sustaining oxygen, but in swift motion becomes deadly tornadoes and hurricanes. Water gives life and enjoyment. But water in swift motion can kill everything in its path. The sea provides us with food but its waves and icebergs have claimed countless victims. If you don't think the sea is evil, watch the movie "Titanic." Fire warms, yet when out of control, it destroys. After hurricane Andrew struck South Florida, I went south to help a friend in need. The area looked as if a hydrogen bomb had flattened it. These powers are all of God.

I am acquainted with evil. My seven year old son, Blake, was bitten by a mosquito and contracted encephalitis. He became comatose. I will never forget the anguish I felt when signing the papers authorizing doctors to remove him from life support. But I will not protect the God I love from any responsibility for evil. God Almighty is the Creator of evil, as is made clear in Isaiah 45:7. *God created mosquitoes that carry the encephalitis that killed my son. I can't deny that. The encephalitis was only the relative cause of my son's death. I don't flinch at the fact that it was God who really took my son. But here's the good news. God knows how painful these evils are that he created. It was no sin on His part to create and use these evils. God uses evil for good. And furthermore, the evils are only temporary. The time is coming when; And there shall be no more curse...* Revelation 22:3. *And God will resurrect my dead son. He will resurrect all the dead.* Job 14:13, 14 (The Message). *And please notice God doesn't just resurrect dead bodies, but dead people. When God removes all evil, no one will suffer again; And God will wipe away every tear from their eyes; there shall be no more death, nor sorrow, nor crying. There shall be no more pain, for the former things have passed away.* Revelation 21:4. *This is the good news that ought to be taught.*

How much more comforting it is to believe the Scriptures. God created evil and uses it for a good purpose. Evil's existence is only temporary, like the scaffolding on a new building. When the building is completed, the ugly scaffolding is removed it serves no further function to the finished building. Only a knowledge of evil, not evil itself has eternal value. How awful to think that God did not foresee the coming of evil, can't justify its existence, can't dispose of it, and can't save most of humanity because of it. There is no justification for, nor redeeming value in eternal torture. None.

God is wise. God wants sons and daughters who will know both "good and evil." God's "end" more than justifies His means. As Paul said; For the momentary lightness of our affliction is producing for us a transcendently transcendent eonian burden of glory..." 2 Corinthians 4:17 Concordant Literal New Testament.

If you do not have a copy of the Concordant Literal New Testament, I would recommend that you get one. The Hebrew Old Testament is not under one cover as yet, but most books are available in paperback. The Concordant Publishing Concern in California has been working on this translation for nearly 100 years. The Greek New Testament was completed back in 1926. When you understand how they translated it, you will see that it is by far the most accurate and consistent translation of the Scriptures in print. You can get a copy through Bible Materials Unlimited 6201 29th Ave. North, St. Petersburg, Fl. 337 10 32 3207. You might also request an eight tape series entitled; Human Choices and the Deity of God by James Coram (the most comprehensive material on "free will" I've ever seen).

Study these marvelous truths. Check the original Hebrew and Greek to verify the validity of what I have humbly tried to present in this letter. The truth concerning the "aions," for example, is one of the simplest truths in the whole Bible to prove and understand that Christ really is the Savior of the whole world! How could anyone ever have a doubt that He would succeed? Who would deny that God Almighty has a heartfelt will? Who would deny that His will involves the salvation of all mankind? 1 Timothy 2:4. *Who can call into question God's declaration that; My counsel shall stand, and I will do all My pleasure...* Isaiah 46:10. *"Falling short" is a definition of "sin" in* Romans 3:23. *God is not going to "fall short" of His own will and thus become a "Sinning God."* **End of quoted article.**

What an amazing introduction to the origins of evil! I thank God for this revelation, even as it continues to challenge and re-shape my understanding regarding God's ongoing redemptive plan for all. I have yet another presentation for you to consider on the purpose of evil, written at the turn of this century by a man named A.P. Adams.

In his forward to this (public domain) work, Brother

Hawtin writes **I quote;** *"For many years I have felt that the gems dug from the mine of eternal truth through the anointed ministry of A.P. Adams, who wrote from about 1885 to 1925, were far too rich to be allowed to be lost to the present generation. I consider it, therefore, to be profitable that I should take in hand the task of compiling some of these precious unfoldings of truth that thousands of others, who have never had opportunity to be edified by his works, may now be blessed by them. God hath set in the Church teachers; but like all other true ministries there are never more than a small handful of them at any given time. We are probably aware that many thousands of men profess to be teachers of the word of God, but in truth they are really merely "warming up" the traditions of the past as a housewife might warm up the leftovers of yesterday. There are many thousands of good musicians in the world, repeating the melodies of the great composers of the past, but they themselves are not composers. So it is with the theologian, if indeed there be such, who re-writes and re-hashes from his own study that which was taught by the ancients. I have often smiled as I have wondered what the common theologian who lived in 1885 must have thought of the truth unfolded by A.P. Adams. I am sure many of them must have thought he was some mad heretic that was only leading mankind astray.*

Our Lord Jesus Christ was received gladly by the common folk of His day. Let us never forget that fact. The publicans and sinners "heard Him gladly" and responded to His message, but the old systems and the old theologians contradicted and blasphemed and never were at rest until they had hung Him upon a cross. Let us always remember that. But truth does not die upon a cross. It lays down its life that it may take it up again in greater power than ever before.

It is with great pleasure that I present this article from the works of A.P. Adams. Sincerely in Christ our Lord, Geo. R. Hawtin." **End of quotation.**

30

The Purpose Of Evil
By A.P. Adams[6]

*T*here is probably no subject in all the range of religious thought so hard to deal with as that of the purpose of evil. Writers on biblical lore have tried to account of the origin of evil; but it seems to me that the real difficulty is the bare fact of its existence, whatever may have been its origin.

The great question for theologians to wrestle with is this: How can you account for the existence of evil alongside a supreme, all-wise, Holy and benevolent God? Think for a moment on the condition of things in this world. Evil exists on the earth to embitter and darken, to blight and curse everything else that exists on the earth. On it goes, like a huge Juggernaut car, rolling through the world, crushing its helpless victims on every hand, and (the saddest feature of all) crushing without distinction the innocent and guilty together in one common quagmire of sin, suffering and death; and God allows it to go on when He might at any instant stop it, and on it has gone for six thousand years.

Take an example in the concrete, the horrible September massacre of the French Revolution when during a period of one hundred hours, from Sunday afternoon, Sept. 2, 1792, until Thursday, the helpless inmates of the seven crowded prisons of Paris were, after a mock trial before a self-constituted tribunal, hurled to a howling mob of human wolves and *fiends and butchered in cold blood. Men and women, young, middle-aged, and gray-haired, shared the same fate, and for no other crime than that, as Carlisle expresses it, they were "suspected of being suspected." And all this was enacted under the canopy of Heaven where sits the God of infinite power and love! How can we believe it?*

Add to this the years of horror of that same revolution. Add the slaughter of the Waldenses and the Albegenses. Add the massacre of St. Bartholomew. Add the unspeakable cruelties of the Spanish Inquisition. Add the decades, centuries and millenniums of butchery and blood that have cursed the world from fratricidal Cain down to the present time, and then try to reconcile all this with the existence in the same universe of a God of infinite power and love! Can you do it? Rather does not the contemplation of this vast sea of human suffering cause one to shrink back with horror from the ghastly vision and almost (and sometimes quite) doubt that there is a God? Alas, how many there are that are troubled by this problem! Can you help them? The Word can help them!

First let me say that there is no help out of this trouble in orthodoxy. In regard to this subject orthodoxy is hopelessly contradictory and utterly absurd. Thus it speaks; "It was not in God's original plan that evil should exist, but evil has come into existence and done incalculable harm; yet God's plans cannot be thwarted nor disarranged in the least, because He is all-wise and almighty. Evil being in existence before man was created, God allows it to come into contact with the man He created when He might have prevented it, knowing full well what the result would be; yet He is in no wise responsible for the consequences of evil. In fact, it is blasphemy to entertain any such idea. Evil having come into existence contrary to God's will, He cannot put it out of existence, but it will continue as long as He exists, an eternal blot on His otherwise perfect universe and a perpetual offense unto all the purified; yet His will is absolute and sovereign and the redeemed will be perfectly happy. Thus, God is in no wise responsible for either the origin, existence, consequences or continuance of evil; yet

He can have everything as He pleases, and is the Creator of all things." And so Orthodoxy goes on, stultifying common sense, throttling human reason, and stupidly expecting that intelligent, thoughtful men and women will accept its idiotic patter as the infallible utterances of divine inspiration. Cannot everyone see that the entire orthodox view is contradictory and absurd in the extreme, and hence self-destructive and untenable?

All Things That Exist Are For an Intelligent And Benevolent End

Now I hold that the following proposition is self-evident. Given a God of infinite power, wisdom and goodness, He is responsible for all things that exist. And this also follows from the wisdom and goodness of God: All things that exist are for an intelligent and benevolent end. These conclusions are inevitable from the premises; they cannot be modified except by modifying the premises. For instance, if you say that some things exist contrary to God's will, then it follows that God is not all-powerful; and you cannot escape this conclusion by bringing in the orthodox doctrine of man's free moral agency, for whatever a free moral agent may do, He is responsible for it who made him a free moral agent. If God made man a free moral agent, He knew beforehand what the result would be, and hence is just as responsible for the consequences of the acts of that free moral agent as He would be for the act of an irresponsible machine that He had made.

Man's free moral agency, even if it were true, would by no means clear God from the responsibility of His acts, since God is his creator and has made him in the first place just what he is, well knowing what the result would be. If God's will is ever thwarted, then He is not almighty. If His will is thwarted, then His plans must be changed, and hence He is not all-wise and immutable. If His will is never thwarted, then all things are in accordance with His will and He is responsible for all things as they exist. If He is all-wise and all-good, then all things existing according to His will, must be tending to some wise and benevolent end. Thus we come back to my proposition again: If God is infinite in power, wisdom and goodness, then He is responsible for all things that exist, and all existing things are tending toward some wise and good end. He who cannot see that this proposition is absolutely inevitable, as much so as a mathematical axiom, must be very deficient in logic and reason, and it would be useless to argue with him.

He who does see the truth of this proposition will also see the truth of several corollaries depending upon it; viz., absolute evil cannot exist because God is absolutely good. The absolute is the unconditioned and unlimited. If there were absolute evil, then the good would be limited, and hence not absolute, and hence again God would not be absolutely or infinitely good. But God is infinite in goodness; hence evil is not infinite. Therefore it is relative, temporary and limited, and therefore again endless evil is an impossibility unless you make God less than infinite. Thus it is seen that the doctrine of endless torments is as contrary to reason as it is to Scripture.

We have arrived then purely by reasoning to the somewhat startling and yet perfectly Scriptural conclusion that; "All things are of God," Ecclesiastes 11:5 *or God is in all things, or is responsible for all things, including all so called evil things as well as good things. Is not such a position as this very dangerous? Is it not a fearful thing to say that evil is of God? I answer there is nothing dangerous or fearful about this view unless the truth is dangerous and fearful. We have seen that reason compels us to this position whether we will or not, and everyone familiar with the Bible ought to know that this view is positively Scriptural. That "All things are of God" is declared over and over again in the Bible. The prophet Amos goes so far as to particularize evil as "Of God" when in his question he makes an implied statement which from an orthodox standpoint would be blasphemous: Shall there be evil in a city, and the Lord hath not done it? Amos 3:6. But what is still more to the purpose, we have the direct positive statement that God creates evil!*

I form light and create darkness; I make peace and create

evil. I, the Lord, do all these things. Isaiah 45:7. This passage is most strange and unaccountable on the ground of any of the current orthodox creeds. God creates evil! It cannot be! But here it is in the word. What will you do with it? "We must explain it somehow," says Orthodoxy, "and yet save our creed. How shall it be done? Suppose we say that the evil here spoken of is not moral evil, sin, or wrongdoing, but physical evil, famines, pestilences, tornadoes, etc., which God controls and sends upon mankind as punishment for their wickedness." It will not do! The word here rendered evil is the one commonly used throughout the Old Testament to denote wickedness, sin, wrongdoing. In some five hundred passages it is so used. For example, see Genesis 6:5; Numbers 14:27; Deuteronomy 31:29; I Kings 11:6; 16:30; Psalms 34:21. The very same word in the original is also rendered "wicked" and "wickedness" more than a hundred times. (See for example Genesis 6:5; 13:13; Psalms 94:23; 101:4). Suppose that instead of trying to explain this passage in harmony with some cut-and-dried creed, we let all creeds go and see if we can find out what the passage really means, and then, if the creed does not harmonize with that meaning, throw the creed away and form a another one that will harmonize with it.

At any rate here is the statement in the word and we will be brave enough to receive it as truth and trust the same One who made it to explain it. Since God is infinitely good and wise and evil is one of His creatures, it must be that evil shall culminate in some good and wise end, as we have already seen. But how can that be? And, if we can by any means understand how it can be, the next question would be what can it be? What can be the end, good and wise, toward which evil is tending?

We can understand how all evil tends to good from the fact that we know from our own experience how some evil tends to good, and in the Bible and in the world around us, we see the same thing illustrated again and again. Now if God has done this in some cases, and if, as we know, He worketh all things after the counsel of His own will, Ephesians 1:11, then it surely is not difficult to believe that He overrules all evil for good. In fact, this must be so, for it is only on this ground, i.e., that all evil tends to be good in the end, that we can harmonize the existence of evil at all with the existence of a God of infinite power, wisdom and love. It is not necessary for us to understand how in each particular case evil is overruled for good in order to believe that it is so overruled. The subject is made still clearer, moreover, from the fact that we can see and understand what some of these good ends are toward which evil conducts us, and thus we come to know something of the purpose of evil. We see furthermore that this purpose is grand and glorious and in perfect harmony with the character of God and that it fully accounts for the existence of evil.

Evil That Brings God's Mercy

How could God ever reveal Himself to man in His mercy, long-suffering, and compassion if it had not been that evil had put us into a position to call for the exercise of these attributes in our behalf? And especially how could God manifest to us His love in all its intensity and greatness except by such an opportunity as evil furnishes? As it is written, In this was manifested the love of God toward us, because God sent His only Son into the world that we might live through Him, I John 4:9 and there could have been no such manifestation of the Father's love if there had been no such thing as evil. We might believe that a friend loved us even though his love had never been especially tested, but we never could appreciate his love unless circumstances transpired to give him an opportunity to exhibit it in all its strength and fullness. So too, we never could understand fully the love of God (and hence never could know Him fully, I Corinthians 13:12, for God is love) had it not been for our lost and wretched condition furnishing the Father with an adequate opportunity for its manifestation.

It was–when we were yet without strength that Christ

died for us. God commendeth His love toward us in that while we were yet sinners Christ died for us. Romans 5:6. *It was because we were in such an evil case, without strength and sinners, that the love that sent the Deliverer is so marked and readily appreciated. Hence "Hereby perceive we the love of God because Christ laid down His life for us." How should we have been able thus to perceive that love in its so great plenitude if we had never come under the power of evil so as to need this extreme manifestation of it?*

Furthermore, as evil gives God an occasion to reveal Himself to us so that we may know Him, so it gives us the opportunity to exercise the attributes of God so that we may become like Him. The existence of evil in the world gives the child of God the opportunity for the exercise of the Godlike attributes of mercy, compassion, forgiveness, forbearance, meekness, and gentleness and thus he becomes like God; for, if ye do these things, ye shall be the children of the highest; for He maketh His sun to rise on the evil and on the good, and sendeth rain on the just and on the unjust, and is kind unto the unthankful and to the evil. Matthew 5:45; Luke 6:35. *Thus we see something of the purpose of evil in the blessings of mankind.*

In addition to all this we have other direct testimony from Scripture that evil is one of God's ministers for good. It is clearly intimated again and again that God uses evil for the accomplishment of His plans, which, of course, are always good. See, for instance Judges 9:23. *Read the context and you will see that Abimelech by a most atrocious crime had obtained the rulership of Israel, and to punish him, "God sent an evil spirit between him and the men of Schechem," and the result was the punishment of all the guilty parties. See the same idea in 1 Samuel 16:14. "The Spirit of the Lord departed from Saul and an evil spirit from the Lord troubled him." This evil spirit did not come from the devil nor from Hell, but from the Lord to do His bidding." See also 1* Kings 22:23; *where the Lord is represented as using a "lying spirit" in order to deceive wicked Ahab for his own destruction.*

The Case Of Job

The case of Job is one of the most striking and perfect illustration of this wonderful truth. The Lord speaks of him as, My servant Job, there is none like him in the earth, a perfect and an upright man, one that feareth God and escheweth evil. Job 1:9. Thus it appears that Job was a remarkably good man, and this is confirmed by Ezekiel 14:14, 20. Now then, what does God do but deliberately hand over this perfect and upright man into the hands of Satan to do his worse upon him, only that he should not touch his life. How could we have a more perfect illustration of how God uses evil as an instrument for good? Although Job suffered intensely, we know that in the end he was greatly blessed by his hard and bitter experience. If God thus uses Satan, the embodiment of evil, as a minister for good in the case of one individual, is it hard to believe that all evil is overruled of God for good in all cases?

The New Testament teaches the same truth. Did you ever notice how strangely the evangelists Matthew and Mark speak of Christ's temptation? The Spirit drove Jesus into the wilderness to be tempted of the devil, and He was there with the wild beasts. Matthew 4:1; Mark 1: 12, 13. What a strange statement! The Holy Spirit of God drives the sinless Jesus into the wilderness among the wild beasts to be tempted of Satan, the arch enemy of all good, a murderer from the beginning, and the father of lies! Truly God creates evil and uses it too, for His own purposes and glory! The apostle Paul fully understood this great truth and practiced it himself. Hence he writes to the Corinthians, To deliver such a one unto Satan for the destruction of the flesh that the spirit may be saved in the day of the Lord Jesus, I Corinthians 5:5 and he declares in his letter to Timothy that he himself had delivered certain ones unto Satan, that they might learn not to blaspheme. I Timothy 1:20. It would seem also that the apostle knew something of this kind of discipline himself, for he says, Lest I should be exalted above measure through the abundance of the revelations, there was given me a thorn in the flesh, the messenger of Satan to buffet me, lest I should be exalted above measure. 2 Corinthians 12:7. *All this clearly proves that God overrules evil for good and that even Satan's work shall result in blessings for God's children.*

Finally, we will notice one more passage more remarkable, if possible, even than those I have cited. In the 20th chapter of the Revelation we have an account of the total restraint of the devil and consequent suppression of evil for a thousand years. What a blessed era of peace and righteousness that will be and how desirable that it should continue and that evil should never again curse the earth! But, lo, wonderful to relate, at the end of the thousand years Satan is loosed out of his prison, and again goes out to deceive the nations, and peace is banished from the earth, and war and slaughter ensues with terrible suffering and destruction.

According to the orthodox idea of the origin and final effects of evil, there would seem to be some terrible mistake here. Either Satan is not watched closely enough, or his prison was insecure, or there was treachery; some awful blunder or more awful crime has been committed to let the devil loose when once he was well secured, surely it would seem from the orthodox standpoint. But so it is not. All is plain when we see the great truth I have tried to set forth in this article. Satan is God's servant to carry out His plans. He is just as much under God's control and works; just as truly under His direction as is the angel Gabriel. God now leaves him free to work out his mischievous will among the children of men. He is the "Prince of this world, John 12:31; 14:30; 16:11 *The spirit that worketh in the children of disobedience.* Ephesians 2:2. *The time will come when he will be bound and put under total restraint and so remain through the Millennium. Then he will be loosed because God has something more for him to do, and he will finally be disposed, but we have seen that evil is needful and beneficial in the end. It is one of God's creatures and His servant, and is conducive to the accomplishment of His gracious plans, as are all other things.*

Thus the Word untangles this great mystery of evil for us and shows us clearly that it is not an interloper in God's economy. It is not a foreign substance in the delicate fabric of God's great plan, obstructing and disarranging its intricate mechanism; nay, it is a necessary part of that plan. It rightly belongs to the marvelous congeries of forces that under the control and guidance of the one supreme mind works and inter-works steadily and without interruption or delay to the glorious end of creating a divine and godlike race. Thank God that on this, as in all other things, He will be glorified and man, in the end, be blessed!

Now, another thought. There are some who say that they could accept the foregoing position if it were not for one thing, the great injustice there is in the world. They can see how God can overrule evil for good in the case of the guilty. Those who deserve punishment are benefited by it, but the evil of this world falls with equal weight upon the innocent as upon the guilty, and even in many cases with greater weight upon the former than upon the latter. The sins of the fathers are visited upon the children. The innocent and helpless suffer most keenly on account of the viciousness and brutality of others, and thus, the most outrageous injustice is perpetrated continually around us in the world. How can all this be permitted in the dominions of a God of absolute justice and boundless love? And how can all this be conducive to good? Is there an answer to this tremendous problem? Two considerations, if I err not, will help us to a solution.

One Purpose Of Evil Is The Development Of Our Character

We have seen that one of the purposes of evil is to develop in our characters attributes akin to God: pity, mercy, compassion, charity, gentleness, etc. Now suppose we lived in a world of absolute justice where no one suffered except what they strictly deserved to suffer, where the innocent never suffered, but only the guilty, and they suffered just so much–no more and no less–as was due to their transgression and as would be beneficial to the transgressor. Suppose we lived in such a world as that. At first thought it would seem as though it would be a very nice kind of world; but how could we in such a world develop the godlike attributes above referred to? There would be no room for heavenly compassion and sweet charity and pity in a world of absolute justice. We would not be likely to pity very much a person who we knew was receiving only the punishment due his fault and that in the end would be for his benefit and blessing. Is it not plain that just this kind of evil, i.e., the evil of injustice, is needed in order that those crowning attributes of God, the tender and loving qualities of our Father in heaven, may be developed and perfected in His human children? Furthermore, so far as the injustice goes, that may be only temporary and apparent. Who shall say that in future cycles which God's plan has yet to run, all the apparent injustice of this present time may not be perfectly adjusted, taken into account, and made right? Surely no one has any right to say it will not be so; and it is perfectly reasonable and probably that it will be so.

But there is still another consideration that fully confirms all the foregoing and still further explains the whole subject. We should always endeavor to discover the underlying principles of God's actions. Nothing that God does is arbitrary or capricious, but every one of His movements has an adequate and righteous cause. He always acts from principle. The outward act may change under different circumstances and toward different individuals, but His principles of action never change. See this whole subject set forth in Ezekiel, chapter forty three. Hence, in order to become acquainted with God, to know Him more and more, we must endeavor to understand, not simply what God does, but why He does it. To know merely what God does is oft time very puzzling and inexplicable. To know why He does it makes all as clear and luminous as noon day. What we need to know, then, in order to know God are the reasons for God's actions, the purpose, "the end of the Lord," James 5:11 the causes and principles of His movements and operations in His dealings with mankind. We may always be sure that there is a just and righteous reason for all God's ways and our endeavor should be to know and understand that reason.

God Uses Evil As An Instrument For Good

Now let us apply this to the subject we are considering. Evil exists, doing things that seem utterly antagonistic to God and His way, but which we are sure from the foregoing considerations to be in some sense of God, in harmony with His will, and conducive to the furtherance of His plans. Now then, is there any principle of action, just and righteous in itself, that will account for the existence of evil and indicate its ultimate result? There certainly is such a principle, thus: It is a recognized principle in law, equity and morals that it is right and just to inflict or permit temporary evil for the sake of an ultimate and permanent good. This principle, all will see is certainly correct. It is upon this principle that all punishment of any kind is justifiable, and it is only on this principle that it can be justified. Punishment is an evil, but it is an evil that may ultimate in good, and when it is inflicted for such a purpose, it is right and just. Now we know from numerous examples, many of which I have given in this article that God acts upon this principle. He uses evil as an instrument for good. Admit that this principle is correct and that God acts upon it, and all is at once accounted for and its final result indicated. This sweeping conclusion may not at once be clear to all, but a little thought will show that it is fully justified. If it is right to use evil as an instrument for good, and if God acts upon this principle, the principle fully explaining and justifying the act, then is it not reasonable to conclude that all evil is so justified? We cannot enter sufficiently deep into God's plans to be able to explain the how and the why of each individual case, but, once admitting the principle, and seeing numerous examples of its application that we can understand, the conclusion is fully warranted that this principle applies to all cases.

Of course, no one could accept this conclusion who believed in endless torment. The above principle will not explain or justify unmitigated and eternal evil. I have already shown that such evil really dethrones God, or at least shares His throne with Him, which is equivalent to dethroning Him. To say that evil is absolute and eternal is to fully invest it with attributes peculiar to Deity and thus to make it "Equal with God" John 5:18; Philippians 2:6. *At least in some respects; but this cannot be. At that rate there would be two gods, a good and a bad one, and each of them would eternally exist and be eternal foes. To such a frightful conclusion does the doctrine of the eternity of evil lead us. Let those believe it who can. But, if we take the Bible teaching on this subject, the principle enunciated fully accounts for and explains the existence and purpose of evil. It may seem to some that this principle cannot apply to all evil. They are able to see how some evil may be overruled for good, but that all the terrible forms of evil can be so overruled seems to them impossible. But such a question is simply one of degree. If God can make some evil conducive to good, can He not so make all evil of whatever form or quantity? If it is true that God uses evil for good at all, how can we tell, not knowing perfectly God's plans and methods, just what kind of evil and just how much evil God will so use? We must conclude that all the evil we see about us in every horrifying form and in all its vast amount comes under the same category of part and parcel of the great plan that through sin, corruption, chaos and death is moving on to holiness, purity, order and life eternal.*

Furthermore, the final outcome of God's plan, so clearly revealed in the Scripture, fully confirms the foregoing view and in fact, irresistibly drives us to that view. All the details and every particular of the plan in all its length and breadth are not revealed, but the result is revealed. And that result, the final outcome, is a perfect and absolute triumph for goodness, truth, and justice. Every knee shall bow and every tongue shall give praise to God. Romans 14:11; Isaiah 45:23. *The whole creation shall be delivered form the bondage of corruption.* Romans 8:21. All *things in Heaven and earth shall be gathered together in Christ.* Ephesians 1:10. *Death shall be swallowed up in victory.* 1 Corinthians 15:54. *There shall be no more anything accursed.* Revelation 22:3. *Every created thing shall praise God.* Psalms 102:18. *This is the outcome! Thank God, it is good enough! To this final result all things are tending. To such a universal victory we are traveling on. We can see it by faith afar off. I cannot doubt that good shall fall at last, far off at last to all. If this is the outcome, then all things, evil included, are to eventuate in good, and thus we arrive at the same conclusion that we have reached in so many other ways in this article. Evil must be done of God's servants for good. It must eventuate in good, for nothing but good is the final result!*

Thus does reason and the Word set forth the purpose of evil. My feeble powers of expression are altogether inadequate for the full presentation of the great truth, but these thoughts will suggest the solution to the problem and will help the lover of truth to a deeper and fuller apprehension of the unique and wonderful ways of God; "Lo, these are parts of His ways; but how little a portion is heard of Him, and the thunder of His power, who can understand!" Job. 26:14. **End of quoted article by A.P. Adams.**

31

Introduction To Hell
And The Lake Of Fire

The following paragraph is a graphic description of a burning Hell that I once believed in and wrote about–based on how I was taught.

"Vast amounts of humanity are perishing as they rush down the broad path of compromise, lavishing upon themselves and others, unspeakable indulgences and pleasures that come forth from the secret chambers of an un-regenerated heart. They know not of their true condition until they arrive at the precipice of no return. The unknowing masses from behind, ever keep pushing forward the ones ahead. Screams of horror can now be heard from those up front while flailing arms and contorted bodies hopelessly try to stop their advancement as the unquenchable heat from within the inferno scorches what very little conscience may be left. Blasphemies against the living God can be heard as those are tumbling into the lake of fire, realize that their name is nowhere to be found written in the Lamb's Book of Life. Too late, too late for the dammed soul! The everlasting smoke from their torment rises upward blotting out all light from the Son."

I thank my loving heavenly Father for rescuing me from the thought of that horrific portrayal of a literal, eternal burning inferno created for the wicked! My fervent prayer is that you too will be rescued from this teaching as well. With that being said, we are challenged to examine the following Scripture passages.

Revelations 21:8; *But the cowardly, unbelieving, abominable, murderers, sexually immoral, sorcerers, idolaters, and all liars shall have their part in the lake which burns with fire and brimstone which is the second death.*

Matthew 10:28; *And do not fear those who kill the body but cannot kill the soul. But rather fear Him who is able to destroy both soul and body in Hell.*

1 Thessalonians 1:9; *These shall be punished with everlasting destruction from the presence of the Lord and from the glory of His power.*

Proverbs 15:29; *The Lord is far from the wicked, but He hears the prayer of the righteous.*

Psalm 11:6; *Upon the wicked He will rain coals; fire and brimstone and a burning wind shall be the portion of their cup.*

Matthew 18:8; *If your hand or foot causes you to sin, cut it off and cast it from you. It is better for you to enter into life lame or maimed, than, rather than having two hands or two feet, to be cast into the everlasting fire.*

Revelation 14:11; *And the smoke of their torment ascends forever and ever; and they have no rest day or night, who worship the beast and his image, and whoever receives the mark of his name.*

These Scripture passages represent a sampling of a few of the more difficult verses that can be found in the Bible. None the less, we must not allow these verses to hinder our journey, so therefore let us proceed!

It is my prayer that the truth as presented in the next four chapters of this book revolutionizes your thoughts, feelings and personal life forever! May your view of others–especially those of your enemies, change so dramatically that out of pure gratitude for what Jesus Christ has personally done for you, cause you to simply come into the total freedom of the living Christ. I am believing that many will be swept into the kingdom of God, as they are set completely free by His un-failing love while it is yet day!

The unconditional love that God has for each of us is not based on what we must do for Him, but rather, what He has already done for us. The love that God has for us and those that will be redeemed from out of that place of utter darkness is, and will be, the most glorious demonstration of God's mercy triumphing over His judgments. It is to this end that all of creation groans for the revealing of the "sons and daughters of God." Let us see how God's ultimate goodness, through the sacrifice of His Son Jesus Christ redeems that which has been lost.

God by His election and calling is redeeming a "first fruits" company, also known as the Bride of Christ through the sacrifice of His Son Christ Jesus, while it is yet day. All others (the majority) are redeemed by that same precious blood, however this will happen beyond the realm of time and space as we know it. Oh how foolish are the ways of man, and how unsearchable are the ways of God past finding out. *"...Father forgive them, for they do not know what they do."*-Words of Jesus Christ.

Lenny and Jan Austin Antonsson are two very special-humble people that the Lord has chosen to use for such a time as this. Through the gift of their writings, they have been able to bring forth in a most wonderful way, the eternal purposes of God for all of humanity. With their permission, I am pleased to present to you a sampling of what Holy Spirit has revealed to them. Enjoy!

32

Send In The Flames
By Lenny Antonsson[7]

*I*n Matthew 3:11, *it speaks about our being baptized in the Holy Spirit and with fire. John said Jesus would come for that purpose. Now, I had no problems with being baptized in the Holy Spirit, but I said to God, "What is the fire for?" And He showed me. "You have been dipped into Me as Savior, Jesus Christ, and you are being dipped into Me as Holy Spirit so that I can lead you into all truth, but you need to be dipped into Me as fire because "I am fire!" The Bible says that, "God is a consuming fire."* Hebrews 12:29. *Yes, I can accept that, but why? What God showed me was that all those whose names are written in the Lamb's Book of Life must be dipped into or baptized with fire, and that fire is the same fire as the lake of fire! This is amazing since we know that all those whose names are not written the Lamb's book of Life will be cast into the lake of fire.* Revelation 20:14, 15. *When I looked up the word for fire in Strong's Concordance, it was as God had said to me. The same Greek word (#4442) is used in both places for fire. In fact, this same word is used in too many Scriptures to include here. Look it up for yourself and you will see what I mean. The Greek word that is translated Hell fire, See* Matthew 5:22; 9:47; Mark 9:43, 47, 48; Acts 2:3; I Corinthians 3:13; 2 Timothy 1:8; Revelations 20:9, 10, 14, 15; 21:8, *(to name a few) for example, is the same one used in*

Hebrews 12:29, *which refers to God as a consuming fire, and also the same as "cloven tongues as of fire" in* Acts 2:3. *Why the need for fire? Because everyone has to be purified with fire before he can stand before a pure and Holy God. That's how simple it is. God is a trinity: Father, Son, and Holy Spirit, or we can also say "Fire, Son, and Holy Spirit", or we can say "Fire, Savior, and Teacher" leading us into all truth.*

God opened my understanding about the purpose of fire, when He spoke to me about being baptized in the Holy Spirit and in fire. In Mark 9:49, *it says; "For every one shall be salted with fire, and every sacrifice shall be salted with salt." Now, this is very interesting because the Church has always led us to believe that only the wicked, the sinners, the unrepentant will be cast into the fire, but in this verse, Jesus says that everyone will be salted with fire. Even the righteous? Even the obedient? Even the saved? Everyone will be salted with fire! This cannot be possible or even reasonable unless fire is for our good; unless it is truly a blessing rather than a place of endless torment which the Church has always threatened us with if we don't repent. What Jesus meant by this statement was foreshadowed in the law, and was pictured there for us to see and to understand.* Leviticus 2:13-15 *reads; "Season all your grain offerings with salt. Do not leave the salt of the covenant of your God out of your grain offerings; add salt to all your offerings." "If you bring a grain offering of first-fruits to the Lord, offer crushed heads of new grain roasted in the fire." Just as Israel was the first-fruits unto the Lord under the Old Covenant,* Jeremiah 2:3 *so we are the first-fruits of the new covenant,* James 1:18, *offered unto God and the Lamb.* Revelation 14: 4.

It is clear that the fire is purging, and refining us, and that's what's taking place in our lives right now. We are being refined by fire. We are being melted down, and the dross is being skimmed off. And later on, those that have not been dipped into the fire are going to have to be cast into the lake of fire and have their dross burned off, because it is impossible for anyone to stand before a pure and Holy God without being refined, without being purified.

I did not see this before, but now, I see it clearly. Now, the reason why I did not see this truth that the fire which Jesus baptizes with and the lake of fire is the same fire that is being used to purify us, is because God had closed off my mind to it. It was not time for me to see it. God's timing is always perfect. He is revealing this to us now so that the fear of Hell, which has been preached by the Church for many, many hundreds of years, can be replaced by the matchless, redeeming love of God! The Holy One of Israel would never expect us to clean ourselves up before we are presented to Him, because He well knows that we are incapable of it. He Himself will do the purifying. He, Himself will present us faultless before His throne with glory and exceeding joy! Jude 24. *Fire is not a fearful punishment! No, it is a glorious deliverance! A cause for rejoicing! Even the lake of fire is a cause for celebration among the lost!*

We have a tendency to confine ourselves to just what we've been taught that the Bible says about a subject. Notice I did not say what it says, but what we've been told it says. Our fear of Hell has made it very difficult for us to allow the Holy Spirit to expand us beyond what we've been taught, and the saints we read about in the Bible were not any different than we are. God allowed them to understand a certain amount and not any more. In fact, the Hebrew writer says that they have had to wait until we "get it" to understand it themselves. Hebrews 11:40. *And now, we are two thousand years beyond that. Who could doubt that the Holy Spirit has expanded our understanding in this past two thousand years? He has not allowed us to remain stagnant, to stand still, and not see additional things.*

However, the Church fears these additional things, these revelations of the Spirit. They forget, or ignore, what Peter said on the day of Pentecost, when he quoted from the prophet Joel; "And it shall come to pass in the last days, saith God, I will pour out of My Spirit upon all flesh; and your sons and your daughters shall prophesy and your young men shall see visions and your old men shall dream dreams; and on my servants and on my handmaidens I will pour out in those days of my Spirit and they shall prophesy." Acts 2:17, 18. *These kinds of manifestations from the Spirit were common place in the early Church. It was the normal operating procedure. Somewhere along the way, among the generations which followed, there grew suspicion about these "extraterrestrial" visitations. Perhaps this was because the Church feared losing control over the people, and could not allow this freedom of expression to continue unchecked. People who spoke from their spirits were often hanged, burned at the stake, and driven out, branded as strange, possessed, or full of the devil, and excommunicated or disfellowshipped. God will not be quenched like that forever, and He will speak to us, whether we feel comfortable with it or not, whether the powers that be allow it or not. God cannot be caged. He will spring forth in glory and in power. The other night, I had a dream, which I offer on its own merits.*

I dreamed about being at some type of convention, where they were building miniature doll houses. I passed one that was very pretty. It was a modernistic doll house. It had no furniture in it, but the paint was beautiful, and right next to it, I started building my own. I built a three or four story high doll house, and I dressed it up with all types of furniture and put beautiful things on the walls, and put very many lovely things inside to decorate it. I stepped aside and looked at it, but I was not satisfied. So, I started another one right next to it, just a small one story house, and I put a person in it, but when I stepped back to view it, I was not satisfied. So, I took the person out and I put him out by himself off to a place at the side, like in a field or a meadow. I looked at the person and I still wasn't satisfied. Then I was in the field, myself, and I stood there and I knew that I was in God, and God was all in all, and I was totally satisfied. I knew I did not need anything else but God. God was my total satisfaction. I had no need for anything else. It was such a blessing to stand there and know that I was completely satisfied with my life because God was the only thing in my life that I had need of. There was nothing else that I needed to carry around, or care for, or be concerned about. I was totally free to be in God all the time.

When the fire has done its cleansing work, we will all be free, and we will be in God all the time! The Father will be in us, and through us, the body of Christ, He will reveal His manifold wisdom, hidden from the ages, unto the principalities and powers in heavenly places. Ephesians 3:10.

That is the end result of the refining fires and the lake of fire as well, that all should come to know the power and the glory and the majesty, the honor, and the wisdom, and the love of the Father as revealed in the Son, through us, His body, now and forever more. Amen. Lenny Antonsson.

33

The Primrose Path To Gehenna
By Jan Austin Antonsson[8]

*(Dedicated to all of my
Grandma Daisy Smith Schumaker's Progeny)*

*B*ut *even if we or an Angel from Heaven should announce glad tidings to you different from what we announced to you, let him be accursed.* (Galatians 1:8, *the Emphatic Diaglott*).

Hell is a four letter word; a topic I'd much rather avoid. In our culture, it evokes either horror or mockery, but rarely indifference. This journal chapter is dedicated to my beloved Grandma Daisy. She was a God fearing, church going, Bible believing woman, but it didn't ease her fears about death, Hell or anything else for that matter. Like many of us, she had been taught that God is severe and His punishments swift and sure. She believed in Hell. I never meant to write about this controversial topic, but I was pressed into it by the Spirit, protesting and groaning all the way. "Please Lord," I moaned. "Don't make me write about this. I don't want to." Now that I have written it, I find, as usual, that whatever He compels me to do has freed me a little more from the ties that bind me. Galatians 3:23.

Decades ago, God began releasing me from the power of sin which comes from the law (I Corinthians 15:56) *and the fear of Hell, by revealing that, "He gives us the victory through our Lord Jesus Christ" (I Corinthians 15:57). Yet in spite of the marvelous revelation of God's grace to my heart, some of Jesus' teachings have troubled me at times because I had no framework to put them in. We have recently acquired several works which shed considerable "Light" on the cultural climate in which Jesus lived and taught. He spoke to ordinary people about the ordinary things they knew about and encountered in their everyday lives. His illustrations and parables are rich with the icons, metaphors and concepts with which they were very familiar. The fact that no one ran screaming into the night when He talked about unquenchable fire* (Matthew 3:12; Luke 3:17) *and the worm that never dies* (Isaiah 66:24; Mark 9:48) *has always amazed me, for in my youth, just reading or hearing about it would make me want to shriek in terror and tear out my hair. The reason why Jesus' audiences didn't react that way is coming right up. Read on.*

A popular saying has it that the primrose path to Hell is strewn with, among other things, good intentions. What I have discovered is that this same path is strewn with misconceptions about it, largely due to inaccurate translations of the word Hell itself and, of course, the political pressure exerted by the Church to maintain control of the flock. As I said, we have come across several books and publications which have illuminated this painful, if not terrifying subject, i.e., everlasting Hell for the damned. God delivered me from this accursed doctrine many years ago, when our dear friend Harry Robert Fox, preached to me, for the very first time, the Gospel of Jesus Christ. This in itself was amazing, since I had attended "gospel meetings" since I was born, but was never delivered from the fear of death and Hell (Hebrews 2:14, 15) *by the message those preachers called the "good news." As a result of those experiences, and the Scriptures which they said proved their point, I have been troubled by certain passages which seem to say just the opposite of what the Spirit of God has impressed upon me to be the truth. Jesus told His disciples that it was necessary for Him to go away, explaining,*

"I tell you the truth: it is to your advantage that I go away, for if I do not go away, the Counselor will not come to you; but if I go, I will send Him to you... when the Spirit of truth comes, He will guide you into all the truth: for He will not speak on His own authority, but whatever He hears He will speak, and He will declare to you the things that are to come" John 16:7, 13 RSV.

Regarding the adulation we see everywhere among believers concerning "The Word of God", by which the person using that phrase means the Bible, let me just say that, God has impressed upon me that Jesus Himself is the Word (John 1:1) of truth (John 14:6). John the Revelator said about Him that "His name is called The Word of God" (Revelation 19:13 KJV). So, I am troubled when zealous Christians refer to the Bible as "The Word" when what they mean is the authority, the dominion, and the reign of God. Jesus Himself is all those things! He is the express image of God, (Colossians 1:15) and in Him are hidden "all the treasures of wisdom and knowledge" (Colossians 2:3).When people ascribe these glorious aspects, which belong only to Christ, unto a written document, they come dangerously close to idol worship, it seems to me. They have "changed the glory of the incorruptible God into an image made like to corruptible man" (Romans 1:23 KJV) and have proceeded to worship a book as life giving, when only Jesus can give us life. (John 6:47, 51, 54-58).

We know, of course, that God's truth is "written not with ink, but with the Spirit of the living God; not on tables of stone, but on tablets of human hearts" (2 Corinthians 3:3 RSV). Why would Paul write that? Because, he goes on to say that our confidence is through Christ, not of ourselves, and not from our own ability to derive truth from a written source. (Romans 7:6). He says, "Our sufficiency is from God, who has qualified us to be ministers of a new covenant, not in a written code but in the Spirit; for the written code kills, but the Spirit gives life" (2 Corinthians 3:4-6). Certainly, I have seen in my own life, that depending on the written word, instead of the Living Word is lethal to Spiritual growth. Jesus encountered this dependence on written Scriptures to find truth throughout His ministry. You can feel His frustration in this passage, "You diligently study the Scriptures because you think that by them you possess eternal life. These are the Scriptures that testify about Me, yet you refuse to come to Me to have life" (John 5:39, 40, NIV). The written word was never intended to be our Source of Light and Truth. The Apostle John wrote, "But the anointing which you received from Him abides in you, and you have no need that any one should teach you; as, His anointing teaches you about everything, and is true, and is no lie, just as it has taught you, abide in Him" (I John 2:27 RSV). Thus, to finish this thought, it seems obvious to me from what the Lord and His disciples said that it is the life of Christ abiding within us Galatians 2:20 that leads us unto all truth, rather than reading the Bible, which leads often times to confusion, disagreement, and much diversity of opinion, if the thousands of denominations who all claim to believe the Bible, are any indication.

We've been hearing about the many errors in the King James Version for some time now, and right after Christmas, we were able to obtain The Emphatic Diaglott, (A) which contains original Greek text, with an Interlinear Word-for-Word English Translation. It states of itself that it is "Based on the interlinear translation, on the renderings of eminent critics, and on the various readings of The Vatican Manuscript." Benjamin Wilson is the man who compiled this translation, and it has become a fascinating reference source for both of us. I quote from the beginning notes here, "King James" Bible, or the Authorized Version, was published in 1611. In the year 1604, forty-seven persons learned in the languages were appointed to revise the translation then in use. They were ordered to use the Bishops' Bible as the basis of the new version, and to alter it as little as the original would allow: but if the prior translations of Tyndale, Coverdale, Matthew, Cranmer or Whitchurch, and the Geneva editors agreed better with the text, to adopt the same. This translation was perhaps the best that could be made at the time, and if it had not been published by kingly authority, it would not now be venerated by English and American Protestants, as though it had come direct from God. It has been convicted of containing over twenty thousand errors."

Certainly, I grew up in an era when, it seemed like most folks believed that the King James Version of the Bible was dropped down from Heaven on a golden thread. Hardly. I've known for a long time that if my eternal salvation depends on getting it right by reading the Bible, then I'd best find a translation with no errors! Since human kind has never produced perfection in anything, that's not a likely event. Another part of the problem is that in 1611, when the King James Version was published, the Church of England exerted enormous influence on its translators, who were admonished not to rock the boat, nor depart from party line, i.e. church authority and accepted orthodoxy. Failure to comply would have been a matter of life and death in those days, since heretics were excommunicated and/or burned at the stake. To say the least, this repressive atmosphere could not possibly have been conducive to absolute intellectual integrity.

I mentioned in the last journal that we have met new friends via the Internet, Gary and Michelle Amirault. They have a Web Site (B) which is a collection of books and tracts, and testimonies, and one of the most fascinating of these is an old work with the less than exciting title of "The Origin and History of the Doctrine of Endless Punishment" by Thomas B. Thayer. It was written in the mid-1800s and, in spite of the forbidding title, I found it fascinating, very scholarly, well researched, and compelling. It is a long work, but well worth reading. For inquiring minds who want to know, this man has exhaustive research to back up his findings.

For instance, the author goes into what I think is one of the most damaging translation errors, one which has deeply affected, and I would go so far as to say terrified, millions of lives over the centuries, and that is the error which led to the doctrine of damnation to Hell fire for all eternity. The author has researched the words which are commonly translated as

Hell. These words are Tartarus and Gehenna, (at last we get to the title of this journal) and I'm going to include a section from the book here to illustrate the flavor of the work. With difficulty, I changed the Roman numerals to their more familiar form.

1. TARTARUS: This word occurs only once, and then in a participial form, in 2 Peter 2:4. *"If God spared not the angels that sinned, but cast them down to Hell, etc." (Tartarosus). This is of the same character with the parable just considered, TARTARUS being the place of torment in Hades, where the rich man* (Luke 16:20-31) *was supposed to be. Bloomfield says that "Tartarus here is derived from the heathen, and chains of darkness from the Jewish mythology;" and adds "it is an expression truly Aeschylean," that is, dramatic, not literally true, a figure of something else.*

2. GEHENNA: This word occurs twelve times in the New Testament, and is always translated "Hell." But as the Evangelists repeat the same discourses, the Savior did not really use it more than six or seven times in all His ministry. The following are the texts: Matthew 5:22; 29, 30; 10:28; 18:9; 23:15, 33; Mark 9:43, 45, 47; Luke 12:5; James 3:6. *By consulting these passages the reader will see how many of them are simply repetitions, and how very few times this word is used, on which, nevertheless, more reliance is placed than on all others, to prove that "Hell" is a place of endless torment.*

The following from Schleusner, a distinguished lexicographer and critic, will show the origin of the word and indicate its scriptural usage: "Gehenna, originally a Hebrew word, which signifies valley of Hinnon. Here the Jews placed that brazen image of Moloch. It is said, on the authority of the ancient Rabbins, that to this image the idolatrous Jews were wont not only to sacrifice doves, pigeons, lambs, etc., but even to offer their own children. In the prophecies of Jeremiah (Jeremiah 7:31) *this valley is called Tophet, from Toph, a drum; because they beat a drum during these horrible rites, lest the cries and shrieks of the infants who were burned should be heard by the assembly. At length these nefarious practices were abolished by Josiah, and the Jews brought back to the pure worship of God* (2Kings 23). *After this they held the place in such abomination that they cast into it all kinds of filth, and the carcasses of beasts, and the unburied bodies of criminals who had been executed. Continual fires were necessary in order to consume these, lest the putrefaction should infect the air; and there were always worms feeding on the remaining relics. Hence it came, that any severe punishment, especially an infamous kind of death, was described by the word Gehenna, or Hell."*

Isaiah says; "They shall go forth, and look upon the carcasses of the men that have transgressed against Me; for their worm shall not die, neither shall their fire be quenched; and they shall be an abhorring unto all flesh." (Isaiah 66:23, 24). *Here the unquenchable fire and the undying worm of Gehenna, or Hell, are used as figures of judgment to happen on the earth, where there are carcasses, new moons, Sabbaths, etc. Gehenna, with its accompaniments, was an object of utmost loathing to the Jew, and came to be employed as a symbol of any great judgment or woe.*

We say of a great military or political overthrow, "It was a Waterloo defeat." So the Jews described a great desolation by a like use of the word Gehenna, "It was a Gehenna judgment" that is, a very terrible and destructive judgment. In Matthew 5:29, 30 *there is mention of the "whole body cast into Hell." No one supposes the body is literally cast into a Hell in the future state. The severity of the judgments falling on those who would not give up their sins is represented by Gehenna which, as Schleusner says, was "a word in common use to describe any severe punishment, especially an infamous kind of death." These wicked people should perish in a manner as infamous as that of criminals, whose bodies, after execution, were cast into Gehenna (Hell), and burned with the bodies of beasts and the offal of the city.*

The same thought is expressed in Matthew 23:33 *where "the damnation of Hell" is a symbol of the tremendous judgments coming upon that guilty nation, when inquisition would be* made for "all the righteous bloodshed upon the earth, from the blood of righteous Abel unto the blood of Zacharias, son of Barachias, slain between the temple and the altar." Matthew 23:34-39.

Mark 9:33, 45, 47 *are repetitions of* Matthew 5:29, 30, *with the addition of "the undying worm and the unquenchable fire," which is a repetition of* Isaiah 66:24. *There is nothing in the passage to show that the Savior used these phrases in any sense different from that of the prophet; who, as we have seen, employs them to represent judgments on the earth, where, "they shall go forth to look on the carcasses of the men who have transgressed against Me ...for they shall bury in Tophet (the place of sacrifice in Gehenna or Hell) till there is no place; ...and the days shall come that it shall no more be called Tophet, nor the valley of the Son of Hinnon, (the Hebrew for Gehenna or Hell) but the valley of Slaughter"* (Jeremiah 7:19-20; Isaiah 66:24).

"Fear not them which kill the body, but are not able to kill the soul; but rather fear Him which is able to destroy both soul and body in Hell." (Matthew 10:28). *Luke says, "Fear Him, which, after He hath killed, hath power to cast into Hell."*

Here is a mixed reference, figurative and literal, to the valley of Hinnon, Gehenna, Hell. There is a literal allusion to casting the dead bodies of criminals into the valley, to be burned in the perpetual or unquenchable fire kept up there for this purpose; but the association of soul and body in the same destruction indicates the figurative use to represent entire extinction of being, or annihilation.

Isaiah employs the phrase in a similar way. "The Lord shall kindle a burning like the burning of a fire, ...and it shall burn and devour His thorns and His briers in one day; and shall consume the glory of His forest, and of His fruitful field, both soul and body" (Isaiah 10:16-18). *Dr. Clarke says this is "a proverbial expression," signifying that they should be "entirely and altogether consumed." So Christ represents God as able to destroy the wicked and apostate, "soul and body in*

Gehenna, the word familiarly used to express any great judgment or calamity" End Quote. (C).

Being from Missouri, I tend to want anyone to "show me," proof of whatever point they are making. So, as I was reading these pages, I thought it would be interesting to get into the Mac Bible computer program we have and print out the references to Hell and look them up one by one in The Emphatic Diaglott. I went through this exercise, and sure enough, in all but two of these passages, the word Hell was translated from the Greek word Gehenna, the word familiarly used to express any great judgment or calamity. (The diligent can compare this list with that of Thayer's on the preceding pages.) List of Scriptures using the word Hell, NIV.

Matthew 5:22; *"But I tell you that anyone who is angry with his brother will be subject to judgment. Again, anyone who says to his brother, "Raca," is answerable to the Sanhedrin. But anyone who says, "You fool!" will be in danger of the fire of Hell" (Gehenna).*

Matthew 5:29; *"If your right eye causes you to sin, gouge it out and throw it away. It is better for you to lose one part of your body than for your whole body to be thrown into Hell." (Gehenna).*

Matthew 5:30; *"And if your right hand causes you to sin, cut it off and throw it away. It is better for you to lose one part of your body than for your whole body to go into Hell." (Gehenna).*

Matthew 10:28; *"Do not be afraid of those who kill the body but cannot kill the soul. Rather, be afraid of the One who can destroy both soul and body in Hell." (Gehenna).*

Matthew 18:9; *"And if your eye causes you to sin, gouge it out and throw it away. It is better for you to enter life with one eye than to have two eyes and be thrown into the fire of Hell." (Gehenna of the fire).*

Matthew 23:15; *"Woe to you, teachers of the law and Pharisees, you hypocrites! You travel over land and sea to win a single convert, and when he becomes one, you make him twice as much a son of Hell, (Gehenna) as you are."*

Matthew 23:33; *"You snakes! You brood of vipers! How will you escape being condemned to Hell?" (Gehenna).*

Mark 9:43; *"If your hand causes you to sin, cut it off. It is better for you to enter life maimed than with two hands to go into Hell, (Gehenna) where the fire never goes out."*

Mark 9:45; *"And if your foot causes you to sin, cut it off. It is better for you to enter life crippled than to have two feet and be thrown into Hell." (Gehenna).*

Mark 9:47; *"And if your eye causes you to sin, pluck it out. It is better for you to enter the kingdom of God with one eye than to have two eyes and be thrown into Hell." (Gehenna).*

Luke 12:5; *"But I will show you whom you should fear: Fear him who, after the killing of the body, has power to throw you into Hell" (D) (Gehenna). "Yes, I tell you, fear him."*

Luke 16:23; *"In Hell, (Hades–unseen), "where he was in torment, he looked up and saw Abraham far away, with Lazarus by his side.*

James 3:6; *"The tongue also is a fire, a world of evil among the parts of the body. It corrupts the whole person, sets the whole course of his life on fire, and is itself set on fire by Hell" (Gehenna).*

2 Peter 2:4; *"For if God did not spare angels when they sinned, but sent them to Hell" (Tartarus), (E) putting them into gloomy dungeons to be held for judgment."While The Emphatic Diaglott is very informative and useful as a tool for study, it would not be my favorite version to curl up with on the coach to read, due to the awkward syntax. Those of us who have studied a foreign language and/or have known one from birth understand the problems which translators have in moving words from one language to another. Here's an example: the NIV translates Matthew 16:18, as follows: "And I tell you that you are Peter, and on this rock I will build My church, and the gates of Hades will not overcome it." The Diaglott word for word translation is: "Also I and to thee say, that thou art a rock, and upon this the rock I will build of Me the Church, and gates of Hades not shall prevail against her." Now, this verse is a case in point of the*

confusion among translations, because the King James renders the passage, "the gates of Hell shall not prevail against it;" the Revised Standard Versions translates it, "and the powers of death shall not prevail against it." So which is right?From the alphabetical appendix of the Emphatic Diaglott, I quote; "Hades occurs 11 times in the Greek Testament, and is improperly translated in the common version 10 times by the word Hell. It is the word used in the Septuagint, (The original Hebrew Bible translated into Greek by seventy scholars, hence called "The Septuagint," B.C. 200-300.) as a translation of the Hebrew word Sheol, denoting the abode or world of the dead, and means literally that which is in darkness, hidden, invisible, or obscure. As the word Hades did not come to the Hebrews from any classical source, or with any classical meaning, but through the Septuagint, as a translation of their own word Sheol, therefore in order to properly define its meaning, recourse must be had to the various passages where it is found. The Hebrew word Sheol is translated by Hades in the Septuagint 60 times out of 63; and though Sheol in many places, (such as Genesis 42:38; I Samuel 2:6; I Kings 2:6; Job 14:13; 17:13, 16, *etc], may signify keber, the grave, as the common receptacle of the dead, yet it has the more general meaning of death; a state of death; the dominion of death. To translate Hades by the word Hell, as is done ten times out of eleven in the New Testament, is very improper, unless it has the Saxon meaning of helan, to cover, attached to it. The primitive signification of Hell only denoting what was secret or concealed perfectly corresponds with the Greek term Hades and its Hebrew equivalent Sheol, but the theological definition to it at the present day by no means expresses it"* (Diaglott, Page 892).

I also printed out all New Testament occurrences of the word Hades which occurred in the NIV. Then I read these from The Emphatic Diaglott. That list is as follows, with the meaning of Hades in parenthesis:

Matthew 16:18; *"And I tell you that you are Peter, and on this rock I will build my church, and the gates of Hades (F) will not overcome it"*

Revelation 1:18; *"I am the Living One; I was dead, and behold I am alive forever and ever! And I hold the keys of death and Hades." (Unseen).*

Revelation 6:8, *I looked, and there before me was a pale horse! Its rider was named Death, and Hades (unseen), was following close behind him. They were given power over a fourth of the earth to kill by sword, famine and plague, and by the wild beasts of the earth.*

Revelation 20:13, *The sea gave up the dead that were in it, and death and Hades (Invisible), gave up the dead that were in them, and each person was judged according to what he had done.*

Revelation 20:14, *Then death and Hades (invisible), were thrown into the lake of fire. The lake of fire is the second death.*

As I was running references here and there, and looking through the Alphabetical Appendix of The Emphatic Diaglott, I chanced across the entry, "Wedding Garment." After I read it, I knew it was no chance encounter, but more of the Spirit's leading me to see beyond what the world and the Church has said the Bible says, into what God wants us to know about these seemingly unknowable mysteries. Matthew 22 recounts Jesus' parable in which He compares the kingdom of Heaven to a king who gave a marriage feast for his son. In this frightening story, the king prepares a lavish wedding feast and sends his servants out to invite the favored guests. Instead of being welcomed, the ungrateful wretches treated his servants shamefully and killed them (Matthew 22:6). Furious at this rejection, the king sent out his troops who destroyed the murderers and burned their city, and then told another group of servants to go out into the thoroughfares and invite as many as they could find. This second group of servants went out and brought in as many people as they could round up, both good and bad (Matthew 22:10) so that the wedding hall was filled with guests. Now here's the terrifying part of the story:

But when the king came in to look at the guests, he saw there a man who had no wedding garment; and he said to him, "Friend, how did you get in here without a wedding garment?" And he was speechless. Then the king said to the attendants, "Bind him hand and foot, and cast him into the outer darkness: there men will weep and gnash their teeth. For many are called but few are chosen." Matthew 22:11-14, RSV.

Even after the Lord showed me through many passages of Scripture and in my heart that His will is being done (Ephesians 1:11) *on earth and that since it is not His will that any should perish* (2 Peter 3:9) *therefore none will,* (Romans 11:32; I Timothy 2:4; I Timothy 4:10; Titus 2:11) *nevertheless, parables such as these triggered the terror I felt as a little girl sitting riveted in the pew while some well meaning evangelist was preaching his version of the Gospel, which he said was the Good News, but which was, in fact, very bad news indeed, i.e. that God is angry; difficult to please; and you're gonna get it big time if you do not obey Him exactly! So, imagine my delight today, when I happened across this reference to the wedding garment in the Appendix of the Diaglott:*

"It was usual for persons to appear at marriage feasts in sumptuous dress, adorned with florid embroidery. But as travelers were sometimes pressed in, and as they could not be provided with such garments, robes out of the wardrobes of the rich were tendered to them. If such persons refused this offer, and appeared in their own apparel, it was highly resented, as a token of their pride and contempt for those who invited them." (Page. 922, The Emphatic Diaglott).

My spirit jumped within me when I read this explanation of what must have been a very common metaphor in Jesus' time, so common in fact, that He didn't bother to explain it at all. He assumed that His listeners would get it. They probably did, but I never did until I read this account. I always thought it was terribly unfair that this poor devil was punished for not having a wedding garment, when he never had any plans to attend the feast until the king's servants dragged him in. Obviously, he did not have a wedding garment with him, or perhaps did not even own one at all. The Lord makes all things plain in His time.

It's easy to see why the above referenced explanation caused the floodlights to go on for me. What does this parable really mean to us reading it two thousand years later? In addition to the obvious inference that the Jews were invited first into the kingdom, but since they stoned the prophets and killed His Son, He invited the Gentiles to come in, I believe the parable means this: God has invited all of us to the marriage feast of the Lamb (Luke 14:15; Revelation 19:9). *From before the foundations of the world* (Ephesians 1:4-11; 2:10; 3:8-11; 2 Timothy 1:9, 10) *He has made elaborate preparations* (I Corinthians 2:9; Isaiah 64:4; 2 Timothy 4:18). *He killed the fatted calf* (Luke 15:23). *He now stands waiting at the door* (Revelation 3:20) *with a ring, a robe* (Luke 15:22) *and a crown* (2 Timothy 4:8; James 1:12; Revelation 2:10) *to welcome us home, but some either don't believe it or perhaps are too busy with things of this world to attend. A few still see God as a despot, waiting to dangle them over the pits of Hell like a spider held over a flame of fire and are therefore too afraid to accept His invitation. Others believe they have to clean themselves up; make themselves worthy; work their way into His favor* (Romans 3:27–28) *so despising the King's offer to provide royal robes for His guests, they are trying to get into the feast wearing their own soiled and ragged wedding garments* (Revelation 3:4, 5). *Isaiah said that all our attempts to make ourselves righteous before God are as filthy rags* (Isaiah 64:6) *a reference to the cloths used to absorb a woman's monthly flux. You can't get a much more disgusting word picture than that, folks, and this vile imagery speaks to what God thinks of our puny, pitiful, and dangerous (G) efforts to earn* (Ephesians 2:8) *what is given as a free gift* (Romans 6:23; 11:29; John 4:10, 14) *paid for by the blood of Jesus* (Romans 3:24, 25) *and provided for us by God's grace!* (Romans 11:6).

God loves us! John 3:16, 17; I John 4:16, 19 *He will never leave us nor forsake us!* Hebrews 13:5. *I believe that the liberating wind of the Spirit is blowing throughout this land, the planet and especially through the Churches to reveal the passionate, undying, never ending love of the Father for His creation. The elect are those whom God has chosen to hear it first, and they in turn will speak this powerful Good News to the Church and then to the rest of creation* I Corinthians 15:22-27. *It is my fervent belief that Hell fire and damnation, the doctrine of endless punishment has done nothing but keep God's precious children chained in the charnel house of fear and rebellion throughout the centuries. That of course, like everything else, was totally part of God's plan* Isaiah 46:10 KJV, *but I wonder if perhaps, now is the time in which He will pour out living water* John 4:14 *to douse the flames of Hell fanned by fear and ignorance. I pray that now is the moment when those who preach endless punishment will begin to speak "The Good News" to those cowering in fear in the pews. Would to God that they would be as passionate and persuasive about the love of God and Christ our Savior, as they have been about the wrath of God.*

Again, this whole issue of endless punishment and Hell fire seems to me more about zeal than knowledge, for the Scriptures declare that our God is a consuming fire! Hebrews 12:29. *He Himself is the fire that John the Baptizer said would come: "I baptize you with water, but one more powerful than I will come, the thongs of whose sandals I am not worthy to untie. He will baptize you with the Holy Spirit and with fire"* Luke 3:16 NIV. *This messenger of the new covenant continues to describe the long awaited Messiah in the next verse: "His winnowing fork is in His hand to clear His threshing floor and to gather the wheat into His barn, but He will burn up the chaff with unquenchable fire"* Luke 3:17. *We usually stop reading there, but let's read the next verse* Luke 3:18, *"And with many other words John exhorted the people and preached the good news to them" Good News, John? Yes indeed. This mighty prophet of God understood something that most of us do not yet see, which is that it is "Good News" that Jesus is the fire that burns off our chaff and burns up the weeds which threaten to choke out our wheat. Why? So that we shall stand perfect before Him! See* Matthew 13:29, 30. *Therefore, my dear friends and family, if you smell smoke and feel the flames scorching your backside, do not despair, and do not worry about what is happening to you. You are experiencing one aspect of God's love! The truth is that like all of God's judgments, Hell is God's refining fire and you don't have to die to reap the benefit of its remedial work. Not only the chaff, but all of our self-effort will be burned up. Paul explains it this way:*

Now if any one builds on the foundation with gold, silver, precious stones, wood, hay, stubble, each man's work will become manifest; for the Day will disclose it, because it will be revealed with fire, and the fire will test what sort of work each one has done. If the work which any man has built on the foundation survives, he will receive a reward. If any man's work is burned up, he will suffer loss, though he himself will be saved, but only as through fire. I Corinthians 4:12-15.

Hell fire and damnation preaching of the fundamentalists, notwithstanding, our God is love! I John 4:16. *And, He is a consuming fire!* I Kings 18:24; Hebrews 12:29. *I've been accused of not believing in Hell fire. Not true. There is a Hell and there is judgment* Acts 17:31; Romans 5:18; Hebrews 9:27; I Peter 4:17; Revelation 20:12. *I've experienced God's judgment many times. Remember, however, that Isaiah said that; "When your judgments come upon the earth, the people of the world learn righteousness."* Isaiah 26:9. *I believe it is in that sense that Peter says; "judgment must begin at the house of God"* I Peter 4:17. *The purpose of it is so that we may learn righteousness. I've felt the flames, smelled the smoke, and received the correction thereof* Hebrews 12:6-7. *If Jesus learned obedience by the things that He suffered* Hebrews 2:10, *why should we, His children, be any different? I've long said that when one who does not know God, passes to the other side, upon entering into the Divine presence, he will feel the pains of Hell as the refining fire does its work. There is not a shred of evidence, however, to suggest that God will punish man forever and ever. That error has to do with another translation problem. The Greek word aionian, which is usually translated as* eternal or forever, actually means "age-lasting." There are excellent discussions of these errors and much more information in The Origin and History of the Doctrine of Endless Punishment. Suffice it to say here that God's love will burn off the dross; the deceit; the sin; the lies; the lust; the pride; the murderous rage and the rebellion, and when the refiner's fire has done its work, all which is left will be of God, through God and to God! Romans 11:36; Ephesians 1:23.

Now that the Father has opened up so many, many Scriptures which reveal His glorious plan, hidden from the ages Romans 16:25, 26; I Corinthians 2:7, the Gospel of Jesus Christ, though which He always intended to bring the Gentiles Colossians 1:26, 27, into His fellowship, I find it incredible that any should imagine that He could possibly fail in this endeavor; that any could think His power so pitifully inadequate to the task; or His will so pathetically impotent, that the devil, a created being, could defeat Him and thwart His eternal purpose. It's unthinkable that God intended that all should be saved and come to the knowledge of the truth I Timothy 2:4, nevertheless, was unable to bring this to pass. The horrible, mind-numbing result that 99% of His children, billions of human beings, will burn in Hell, forever separated from the love of the one responsible for bringing them into the world, is absurd. It is ghastly horror, insupportable error, and blasphemous to the power and authority of Almighty God!

In recent years, I heard a woman say about everlasting punishment, "Well, that's what the Bible says." My quick reply is, "No, that is not at all what the Bible says. That is what the Church says the Bible says." The Bible is like a gold mine. You've got to dig through a lot of layers of rock to get to the goodies. In His time, God lets you in on His secrets, here a little, there a little, line upon line, precept upon precept Isaiah 28:10, 13. In his article entitled, "Orthodoxy," (F) A.P. Adams writes, I quote;

"If everything in the Bible was plain and simple like a child's primer, it would require no effort to receive it, and hence, though we might obtain a certain number of truths, *there would be but very little spiritual training. An order of men is now being fitted and trained to be the kings and priests of the "ages to come," the promised seed in whom all the families of the earth are to be blessed; the sons of God for whom the whole creation waits* Romans 8:19, *and this order must reach the perfect man condition by a gradual growth and development... To them it is given to know the mysteries of the kingdom of Heaven; but to those who do not belong to this order it is not given, because they do not need to see these deep things of God yet. But they shall see in the judgment age when the inhabitants of the world shall learn righteousness* Isaiah 26:9.*Thus taking God's plan into consideration, the apparently dark, puzzling, and mysterious character of the Word is fully accounted for and clearly shown to be but another manifestation of that "wisdom and knowledge of God," the depths of which are unsearchable and past finding out* Romans 9:33. *Pg. 108. End of quotation.*

Pardon my cynicism, but I'll remind myself and anyone else who may have forgotten, that the Roman Catholic Church made a fortune in the dark ages by selling indulgences, the primary purpose of which was so people could buy their loved ones out of purgatory, the waiting room of Hell. Hell was good for business, for at that moment, Church was a business and the woman, symbolizing God's people, had long been riding the Scarlet beast, representing the world's system Revelation 17:1-18. *Hell is still good for business, actually. Church leaders are ever fearful that if people learn that God loves them unconditionally, they will escape the control which pastors and elders love to exercise, for the good of the flock, of course. Fear may not be the best motivator, but it keeps the kids in line and insures that the parishioners keep coming, giving, and serving.*

Some will not get this truth, on this side of the veil, no matter how gifted the teacher or how diligent the search, for God has always hidden truth from the wise Matthew 11:25; Luke 10:21; I Corinthians 1:19-21, *and revealed it to the simple. When Jesus disciples asked Him why He spoke in parables,*

He replied; The knowledge of the secrets of the kingdom of Heaven has been given to you, but not to them. Whoever has will be given more, and he will have an abundance. Whoever does not have, even what he has will be taken from him. Matthew 13:11, 12.

Though this is disconcerting, and not what most preachers want to hear, nevertheless, John the Beloved declared that Jesus "was the true Light, which lighteth every man that cometh into the world" John 1:9. *See also* John 1:29; 3:17; 6:33; 1 John 2:2; 4:14. *Note that the Apostle says; "every man." In* I John 2:2, *He asserts, "And He is the propitiation for our sins; and not for ours only, but also for the sins of the whole world" There is no time limit and no qualifiers on these prophecies. Paul said; that every tongue would confess and every knee would bow to the Lordship of Jesus Isaiah* 45:23; Philippians 2:10, 11, *and there's no time limit on that promise nor any indication whether it will happen here or "over there." This is why I believe that some will hear the Gospel on "this side" and some on "the other side" of Jordan. John the Revelator proclaimed, "And I saw another angel fly in the midst of Heaven, having the everlasting gospel to preach unto them that dwell on the earth, and to every nation, and kindred, and tongue, and people"* Revelation 14:6. *What I believe passionately is that when an unbeliever passes into the presence of the living God, and encounters Him face to face, he will then know as he is known; his eyes will be opened and his ears unstopped, and he will encounter a love that will not let him go; a love so white hot and passionate that it will burn off the dross, the chaff, and everything carnal in him. Everything in the universe that exalts itself above the throne of God will be brought down to the sides of the pit Isaiah* 14:13-15. *Malachi penned these thrilling words; Behold, I will send My messenger, and he shall prepare the way before Me: and the Lord, whom ye seek, shall suddenly come to His temple, even the Messenger of the covenant, whom ye delight in: behold, He shall come, saith the Lord of hosts. But who may abide the day of His coming? and who shall stand when He appeareth?*

For He is like a refiner's fire, and like fullers' soap; And He shall sit as a refiner and purifier of silver: and He shall purify the sons of Levi, and purge them as gold and silver, that they may offer unto the Lord an offering in righteousness. Malachi 3:1- 3.

Thinking about that verse, I strongly suspect that when the Lord comes to His temple, where He is even now, none of us shall stand when He appears. Like Ezekiel (Ezekiel 1:28), Daniel (Daniel 8:17) Paul (Acts 9:4) and John, (Revelation 1:17), we will all fall flat on our faces before Him. We'll laugh and we'll cry and we'll praise and we'll soar, for "when He appears, we shall be like Him, for we shall see Him as He is" I John 3:2. So in "Light" of this glory, what's a little pain? A little privation? A little suffering? A little depression? Nothing at all, Paul assures us, compared to the eternal weight of glory which shall be worked into us 2 Corinthians 4:16, 17. *And not only us, but all men will share in God's bounty: Listen to this Good News:*

For the grace of God has appeared for the salvation of all men, training us to renounce irreligion and worldly passions, and to live sober, upright, and godly lives in this world, awaiting our blessed hope, the appearing of the glory of our great God and Savior Jesus Christ, who gave Himself for us to redeem us from all iniquity and to purify for Himself a people of His own who are zealous for good deeds. Titus 2:11-15, RSV.

What can make good news even better? "The Zeal of the Lord of Hosts will perform it" 2 Kings 19:30, 31; Isaiah 37:32. *He promised it through the prophets, and He will deliver. So, buckle your seat belts and get ready for the most glorious ride of your lives!*

Now unto Him that is able to keep you from falling, and to present you faultless before the presence of His glory with exceeding joy, to the only wise God our Savior, be glory and majesty, dominion and power, both now and ever. Amen. (Jude 24, 25. KJV).*The graphic on the title page (of this article–not shown here) shows a little devil dancing in the flames of Hell.*

I smiled when I first saw it, because in my opinion, the devil is the only one who deserves the traditionally depicted flames of Hell. Jesus said in Matthew 25:41, *"He will then also say to those on His left hand, 'Depart from me, you cursed ones, into that aionian (age lasting) fire, which is prepared for the adversary and his messengers." John the Revelator observed; And the sea gave up those dead which were in it; and death and Hades (the unseen) gave up the dead which were in them; and they were judged each one according to their works. And death and Hades (the invisible, in the literal Greek) were cast into the Lake of Fire. This is the second Death, the Lake of Fire.* Revelation 20:13, 14.

This verse alone proves that Hell is not everlasting, not forever. John prophesied that it will give up the dead in it and be destroyed in the lake of fire. If one person gets out of Hell, then surely all have hope of such deliverance. No one resigned and appointed me "pope" in order to interpret the things of the Spirit for anyone else I Corinthians 2:11-13. *The information in this journal has clearly been for my own redemption, but I gladly offer it and the Scriptures therein to anyone else who resonates to it, no strings attached. As for me and my house, I'll take comfort from* Psalm 36:5, 6, *which reads; Your love, O Lord, reaches to the heavens, your faithfulness to the skies. Your righteousness is like the mighty mountains; your justice like the great deep. O Lord, you preserve both man and beast. How priceless is your unfailing love. Both high and low among men find refuge in the shadow of your wings.*

Let him who has an ear hear. The Lake of Fire is God Himself! And who knows, it just may be that when he gets that close to God, even the devil will get the Hell burned out of him and enjoy a second chance. By Jan Austin Antonsson. Notes. [9]

34

Hell Is A Four Letter Word
By Jan Austin Antonsson[10]

*The following was given as a devotional at Medicalodge,
Neosho, MO, on Feb. 4, 2001.*

*I grew up in a Church right here in Neosho that believed
in Hell fire and eternal damnation. Worse, they believed
that anyone who wasn't in their Church, was going to Hell
when they died. That includes a whole lot of folks, probably
most of us in this room today, if they were right. Thank God,
they were not! When I was a kid, I asked one of the elders
who was teaching my Sunday School class about the folks
in Africa, let's say, who never, ever heard the name of Jesus,
nor had any way to hear about Him. "Will they burn in Hell
when they die?" I asked, because that seemed horribly unfair
to me, even as a child. He answered, sadly, "Well, yes, Jani,
but we just don't understand these things." No, I guess not. It
worried me terribly because some of my cousins didn't go to
Church and I knew that meant they would be "toast" if they
didn't repent before they died. I read the Bible daily to try
to find out the answers, but the trouble was, I only saw the
Scriptures the leaders used to prove their points, and missed
the ones which disproved them. God stepped in and delivered
me from this terrible teaching. When I was about 25 years old,
I met a man in California, Harry Robert Fox, who was the son
of a Church of Christ missionary to Japan, and who himself*

had been a Church of Christ missionary to Japan for many years. He shared the gospel of Christ with me for the first time, which is that ultimately, God is going to save everyone. Now, before you get all riled up, and ready to stone me, let me go on with my journey into truth. It is my journey, and I'm not trying to sell my conclusions to you, but rather, just report them to you. You can make up your own mind about it after you have heard what I have to say, and hopefully, you'll look up the many Scriptures I have included here.

Harry's statement about God saving everyone found a home in my heart, because I could never figure out how to love a God who would fry you in Hell if you didn't obey the rules, considering that no one agreed on what those rules were anyway. Once I accepted the truth of the gospel message, regarding God's plan of the ages, the Scriptures started to leap out at me. Here are a few of them: The Apostle Peter, under the anointing of the Holy Spirit, wrote; "The Lord is not slack concerning His promise, as some men count slackness; but is long-suffering to us-ward, not willing that any should perish, but that all should come to repentance" 2 Peter 3:9. "Wow," I thought, "if God is not willing that any should perish, then how could anyone perish?" But, you know, it seems to me that some Christians act like they believe God's glory days were mostly in the Old Testament when He was fierce and vigorous, mighty and valiant. He sent armies here and angels there to defeat the enemies of Israel, and no one could stop Him. They also know that He did mighty works when Jesus walked the earth, but some appear to think that He grew old and tired along the way. I got a mental picture of how some folks see Him, sitting in His wheelchair in some celestial retirement home for weary gods, too tired and feeble to do much of anything anymore, except throw people into Hell if they disobey the rules. That's pathetic, and certainly not true! Long ago, the prophet Isaiah declared; "Behold, the Lord's hand is not shortened, that it cannot save; neither His ear heavy, that it cannot hear" Isaiah 59:1. Today, in 2001, this is still true of Him. The answer to the question, "Is God

*so weak and feeble that He can't get His will done on earth?"
is found in* Ephesians 1:11, *where the Apostle Paul affirms
that God, "works all things after the counsel of His own
will." My heart leaped within me. Listen to it again. This
verse says; "He works all things according to His own will."
Not my will or your will or some Church leaders will, but His
will! That put a new slant on things entirely.*

*Too often preachers and televangelists still threaten us
that if we don't "obey the gospel, we will burn in Hell." How
many sermons have we all heard like that? I suppose they
think they are doing us a favor by scaring us toward God,
but it is entirely the wrong approach, which really has just
the opposite effect. There surely can't be even one person in
America who hasn't heard about Hell, and yet our prisons are
overflowing and Church attendance is at an all time low. The
threat of Hell may have kept some timid types from committing certain sins, but in fact, it has turned millions away from
Church and our loving Heavenly Father. They want nothing
to do with a god who will burn the majority of His children
in Hell for all eternity. We have an Internet Ministry, and a
goodly number of these wounded and disillusioned folks are
expressing themselves out there in Cyberspace, and often, they
find our Glory Road website (link at the end) and write to say
how blessed they are by our writings.Religion's whole deal
about avoiding Hell is for man to do something in response
to God's invitation, rather than understanding what God has
already done in Jesus Christ. Each Church has a different spin
on what man needs to do, and I don't want to "go there" right
now, but let me talk about the one step that is at least part
of everyone's formula for salvation.* Acts 2:21 *and* Romans
10:13, *both say; "For whosoever shall call upon the name of
the Lord shall be saved." Now, most everyone adds something
to that, but let's just take it by itself for now. The Apostle
Peter in Acts and the Apostle Paul in Romans said that whoever calls on the name of the Lord shall be saved. Who am I
to argue with two Apostles?*

From there, the Spirit led me to Philippians 2:10, 11 *which declares, that at the name of Jesus every knee should bow, in Heaven and on earth and under the earth. And that every tongue should confess that Jesus Christ is Lord, to the glory of God the Father. What hit me immediately, when God shined the "light" of His Spirit on that passage was that it says, every knee and every tongue, and goes further to say, in Heaven, and on earth, and under the earth. Remember, that the ancients believed that the place of the dead, Sheol, (the Hebrew word) was under the earth. So Paul says that every tongue and every knee of those on earth, in Heaven, and under the earth, (the dead), will confess that Jesus Christ is Lord. Putting that together with the verse that says whoever calls upon the name of the Lord shall be saved, it's an easy step to the conclusion that all will be saved. There are actually over 100 Scriptures which declare the truth that all will be saved, but let's just include one more here: I John 2:2; "And He is the propitiation for our sins: and not for ours only, but also for the sins of the whole world." The word "propitiation" means "to make favorably inclined, to conciliate."*

These are but a few of the Scriptures which led me to believe as I do that no one will burn in Hell forever and ever, but now, I want to talk about the word "gehenna," which is translated "Hell" in many Bibles today, including the King James version. "Hell" is a mistranslation of the Greek word, "Gehenna," which refers to the Valley of Ben Hinnom 2 Chronicles 28:3; Jeremiah 7:32, 33; 32:35. *It was a literal place where refuse, carcasses of dead animals, bodies of criminals and other detritus of their lives were thrown to be burned up. The fires burned continuously, in order to dispose of the waste and keep germs under control. It was a place of horror to the Jews in Jesus' day, and this was the metaphor Jesus used in several passages when He describes it as a place, "where 'their worm does not die, and the fire is not quenched"* (Mark9:48). *If you look at a Greek New Testament, like The Emphatic Diaglott, you can see that in almost every place the word "Hell" is used, it is translated, "Gehenna."*

My husband Lenny and I drove through the Hinnom Valley

Gehenna still located southwest of the old City of Jerusalem, when we visited Israel in March, 2000, and our Israeli tour guide joked, "Now, you can go home and tell your friends that you went to Hell and back." Without doubt, Gehenna was an EPA nightmare, but it had nothing to do with the afterlife. It symbolized judgment on this earth, and Jesus used it as a metaphor (figure of speech) to make a point about righteous living here and now, not our eternal destiny after we die. I wrote an in-depth article on this, entitled; "Primrose Path to Gehenna."

The professing Church has held our feet to the fires of an everlasting Hell, dear ones, because it has been good for business. This pagan doctrine, which originally came out of Egypt and Babylon, is used to keep Church attendance up, cause money to flow into the contribution baskets, and insure that Church leaders have the "proper" control over the flock. But, let's get real here. Hell may have kept a certain fearful few from doing some terrible things, but it never helped any of us to love God or each other. In fact, I would be so bold as to say, that if you are commanded to love God as the only way to avoid Hell, you'll lie and say you do, when really, you want to run screaming into the night tearing out your hair along the way.

I want to make one last point here about what Paul calls the mystery of the gospel Romans 6:25; Ephesians 6:19. In Ephesians 3:6, *he explains this mystery, hidden from the foundation of the world. There, he says; "That the Gentiles should be fellow heirs, and of the same body, and partakers of His promise in Christ by the gospel." I've been praying and meditating on this topic all week, to be sure not to miss what God would have me share with you today. When I woke up Friday morning, He brought something into focus for me that I'd never seen quite this way. In* Ephesians 2:12, *the Apostle Paul wrote; "That at that time (before Christ paid the price for us) you were without Christ, being aliens from the commonwealth of Israel, and strangers from the covenants of promise, having no hope, and without God in the world." I mentioned to you on another occasion, that all of us would have fallen into the Gentile category. The Bible is basically the story of God's creation, of His covenant promise to Abraham* Hebrews 6:13, *that in Him, all nations would be blessed* Galatians 3:8, *and of His plan from before the foundation of the world to restore and redeem His creation* Acts 3:21; Romans 16:25; I Corinthians 2:7; Ephesians 3:5, 9; Colossians 1:26; Titus 1:2. *In Bible times, there was only one true religion, the Jewish religion, because there was only one true God, the God of Abraham, Isaac, and Jacob. The other people on earth were aliens from the commonwealth of Israel, strangers from the promise, with no hope and without God in the world. Today, we've got thousands of different Christian denominations, plus Muslims, Hindus, Buddhists, and many, many more.*

The proliferation of religions keeps us from seeing the simple truth that the Bible portrays. In terms of Paul's doctrine, there were only two types of people, Jews and Gentiles. Jews had a covenant relationship with God because of His promise to Abraham, but the Gentiles were completely out in the cold before Christ came. They had nothing. Christ came and broke down the middle wall of partition between Jew and Greek, righteous and unrighteous, and brought those of us (Gentiles) who were far off, nigh unto God by the cross. Ephesians 2:13, 14.

No wonder the Jews hounded the Apostle Paul from city to city, beating and stoning him, and blaspheming him everywhere he went. They didn't want to share what they had with "those low class" sinners, the Gentiles, which includes all of us, of course. Sadly, many Christians feel the same way about the unsaved. They don't want to associate with sinners lest they be contaminated. Jesus said of Himself that He came eating and drinking and was scorned and ridiculed as a "winebibber and glutton, a friend of publicans and sinners." Matthew 11:19; Luke 7:34. *Jesus was, "the true Light, which lighteth every man that cometh into the world"* John 1:9. *This includes Jews and Greeks, nerds and geeks, blacks and whites, and Afghanites, Europe, Asia, Africa, all. God loves everyone, short and tall. Jesus came to seek and save the lost, which included everyone!* Luke 19:10. *Yes, it is true that "Our God is a consuming fire,"* Hebrews 12:20 *but He is also love* I John 4:8, 16. *All of us were sinners when Christ came. None were righteous, no not one* Romans 3:12. *One last passage and then we're done here: "But God commendeth His love toward us, in that, while we were yet sinners, Christ died for us. Much more then, being now justified by His blood, we shall be saved from wrath through Him. For if, when we were enemies, we were reconciled to God by the death of His Son, much more, being reconciled, we shall be saved by His life"* Romans 5:8-10. *No one has to fear God. He loves us and it is a promise all through the Bible, when your spiritual eyes are opened to see it, that He will restore all things to Himself* Acts 3:21. *He was never angry at us; we were angry at Him, and Jesus came to reconcile us back to the Father's bosom* 2 Corinthians 5:18. *He came to bring us eternal life* John 17:3. *Hallelujah.*

Hell really is a four letter word, the scariest word that I've ever heard. (Matthew 25:46; II Thessalonians. 1:8) *But God has a secret, which is too good to keep.* (Matthew 13:11, 13, 34-35; Amos 3:6) *When you listen with your spirit instead of your ears,* (I Corinthians 2:12-15) *you hear the truth, which has been hidden for years.* (Romans 16:25; I Corinthians. 2:7; Ephesians. 3:5, 9; Colossians. 1:26; Titus. 1:2) *God is not weary, weak, or faint. There isn't any place at all, where He is not.* (Ephesians. 4:6) *"If I make my bed in Hell," the Psalmist cheers, God is there too, calming my fears.* (Psalms 139:8)

We call on the name of the Lord to be saved, (Acts 2:21; Romans. 10:13) *even those whose sin keeps them enslaved.* (Romans. 5:8; Hebrews. 9:26) *"Every knee shall bow; every tongue confess,* (Romans 14:11; I John. 4:15) *that Jesus is Lord,"* (Philippians 2:11) *and thus, all shall be blessed. It's impossible to believe our Father could fail leaving most of His children to burn in Hell. God sent His only begotten Son to save all in the world, every last one.* (John 3:16-17; I Corinthians. 15:21-22; I Timothy. 4:10; Titus. 2:11) *His hand is not shortened, that He cannot save;* (Isaiah 50:2; 59:1; II Peter 3:9) *The Church says it's only for those who behave, but before the world ever began, God had a plan.* (Matthew 25:34; Ephesians 1:4; 2:6; I Peter 1:20; Revelation. 13:8) *It was "Jesus, the Lamb slain" to save every man.* (John 1:7, 9; 12:32; Romans 5:18; Hebrews 9:26; I John 2:2) *Hell is for the Devil and his motley crew,* (Matthew. 25:41) *it was never meant for me and you.* (Hebrews 2:14; I John 3:8) *"The Victory is ours," thus saith the Lord.* (Isaiah 25:8; I Corinthians 15:54, 57; I John 3:8; 5:4) *Our destiny rests on His glorious Word.* (Deuteronomy 8:3; Isaiah 40:5; 58:14; Hebrews 11:3; I John 2:14; Revelation 19:13) *He called us from a world of sin and strife.* (Ephesians 2:1-7, 12) *He gave us His name* (James 2:7; II Timothy 1:12) *and eternal life!* (John 10:28; Romans 5:21; 6:23; I Timothy 6:12; Titus, 3:7; I John 1:2; 2:25; 5:13, 20). *Jan Antonsson.*

35

The Other Side
Of The Lake Of Fire
By Jan Antonsson[11]

Given for the Saints at Medicalodge, Neosho, MO, on 3/7/04

*B*ut *the anointing which you received from Him abides in you, and you have no need that any one should teach you; as His anointing teaches you about everything, and is true, and is no lie, just as it has taught you, abide in Him.* I John 2:27, RSV.

The following essay is in response to a brother's question about a writing I sent to him entitled; "The Lake of Fire and Brimstone," by John Gavazzoni, available upon request. He wrote; "Jan, I truly want to believe this doctrine of Ultimate Reconciliation. And I was ready to agree with the Lake of Fire deal. But how do you explain Revelation 20:11-15; Revelation 21: 8; Revelation 21:27; *and* Revelation 22:1-15? *I understand your insights into biblical fire and I agree with them. But why didn't John the Revelator make it perfectly clear in the above passages. It seems to end in "Limbo" and not in this great "Ultimate" conclusion. Love ya, Jake." (Not his real name).*

Dear Jake, Here are the Scriptures you ask about. I am asking the Lord to give me clarity as He reveals their meaning for us today.

1) Revelation 20:11-15; *Then I saw a great white throne*

and Him who sat upon it; from His presence earth and sky fled away, and no place was found for them. And I saw the dead, great and small, standing before the throne, and books were opened. Also another book was opened, which is the book of life. And the dead were judged by what was written in the books, by what they had done. And the sea gave up the dead in it, Death and Hades (unseen) gave up the dead in them, and all were judged by what they had done. Then Death and Hades were thrown into the lake of fire. This is the second death, the Lake of Fire; and if any one's name was not found written in the book of life, he was thrown into the Lake of Fire. RSV.

This passage has been used to scare people up to the altar for centuries, no doubt, but when you see it with your spiritual eyes open, it's actually very comforting. Hades is one of the words translated "Hell" in the King James Version. Jonathan Mitchell translates it simply as "unseen." Here's verse 13 in the KJV; *And the sea gave up the dead which were in it; and death and Hell delivered up the dead which were in them: and they were judged every man according to their works.* Notice that death and Hell delivered up the dead which were in them, proving that whatever Hell is, it is NOT everlasting, forever and ever, for the dead in there got out. Remember that Jesus went to the souls in prison (Hades/Sheol) in Noah's day, and preached the gospel to them I Peter 3:18-20. They got a second chance after death, and if they did, how can we say that no one else will? And also, if Jesus preached to them, do you think they refused Him?

Revelation 20:15, *in the King James Version, tells us that death and Hell were cast into the lake of fire, again proving that Hell does not last forever. It ends in the lake of fire, which Scripture tells us is God Himself! Our God is a refining fire* Hebrews 12:29. *It is where the dross is burned off, the hay, wood and stubble burned up, the works of our hands not built on the foundation of Christ will be consumed by this fire, but Paul assures us, If any man's work is burned up, he will suffer loss, though he himself will be saved, but only as through fire.* I Corinthians 3:15, RSV. *Do you see the good news here? It's bad for those who plan to build up a credit in the first bank of Heaven against which they can slide past a few sins, for those of us who depend on grace alone to get us there, its wonderful news.*

2) Revelation 21:8; *But as for the cowardly, the faithless, the polluted, as for murderers, fornicators, sorcerers, idolaters, and all liars, their lot shall be in the lake that burns with fire and sulfur, which is the second death. RSV. Here again, we have good news about the fire and sulfur (cleansing agent) used to burn off the dross, which these sins represent, and both Lenny and John Gavazzoni have pointed out that a man who does these things has never met Christ and therefore does not know who He is. He is acting out of unbelief and ignorance, but when he sees Christ, he will be changed. My personal conviction is that when he is immersed into the lake of Fire, which is God Himself, he will see Him as He is and then he will be like Him. We are all children of God, but some do not know this yet because God has not revealed Himself to them.*

As I was meditating on this verse, the Lord showed me that the second death is in fact, the death of death. It is the end of the flesh. My grandfather is quoted as saying that we begin to die the moment we are born. When He came in the flesh, Christ entered the death realm with us, but He took it to the cross with Him. Paul said of His death, the death He died He died to sin, once for all, but the life He lives He lives to God. Romans 6:10, RSV. *Christ delivered us from the sting of death and the power of law to kill, once and for ALL. In an e-mail dialogue with Jonathan Mitchell about this, he wrote a much appreciated summation of this misunderstood topic of the second death."The lake of fire eliminates death, and the realm of death, (Hades/Sheol) as well as the adversarial spirit, (the Devil/Satan) false speaking (false prophet) and the beast nature* Revelation 20:10, *and our works of wood, hay and stubble." Only God could take something as frightening to the human mind as fire and brimstone, and turn it into such incredibly good news!*

3) Revelation 21:27; *But nothing unclean shall enter it, nor anyone who practices abomination or falsehood, but only those who are written in the Lamb's book of life. RSV. Here again, anyone who is immersed into the Lake of Fire will have the dross burned off, and there will be nothing unclean left in him. We mud creatures are like a diamond, which is really a lump of coal. When it is subjected to millions of years of heat and pressure, it becomes a sparkling, valuable, beautiful jewel. Malachi spoke of this in powerful symbolic terms: But who can endure the day of His coming, and who can stand when He appears? For He is like a refiner's fire and like fullers' soap; He will sit as a refiner and purifier of silver, and He will purify the sons of Levi and refine them like gold and silver, till they present right offerings to the Lord. Then the offering of Judah and Jerusalem will be pleasing to the Lord as in the days of old and as in former years.* Malachi 3:2-4, RSV.

Notice that God is referred to as a refiner's fire (there it is again) and fullers' soap, (a bleaching or cleansing agent) used to purify the sons of Levi (the priestly tribe, which we are in Christ, Revelation 1:6) *and refine them like gold and silver. I'm sure you know that unrefined gold and silver ore is heated to the boiling point, and when the dross comes to the top of the boiling metal, it is skimmed off leaving a pure product behind. The end of the process of purification is that Judah and Jerusalem (a type of the elect) will be pleasing to the Lord again. In fact, Ezekiel said; that even wicked Sodom, which was totally destroyed by fire and brimstone falling from Heaven,* Genesis 19:24; Deuteronomy 29:23, *would be restored and returned to her former estate* Ezekiel 16:53, 55. *Hallelujah for the cleansing fire!*

4) Revelation 22:14-15; *Blessed are those who wash their robes, that they may have the right to the tree of life and that they may enter the city by the gates. Outside are the dogs and sorcerers and fornicators and murderers and idolaters, and everyone who loves and practices falsehood. RSV. Here again, the ones outside the gates, the ones who do not have*

access to the tree of life, are those who have not yet been cleansed, but remember that all of us fell into this category until we were Baptized in Holy Spirit. Then we had the eyes of our understanding opened to see the plan of the ages unfold in our lives. John the Baptist prophesied that the one coming after him would baptize them with Holy Spirit and with fire! Matthew 3:11; Luke 3:16. *This is a promise, not a threat. The faithful Jews were looking forward to it because they understood the significance of both.*

The answer to your question about why John the Revelator was not clearer in his message to modern readers, is that he was writing in symbols so the Roman authorities would not understand him. It was a capital offense in Rome to be a Christian and worship the true God, for Caesar was considered god, and anyone not worshipping him was condemned to death. John knew that the Christians who were filled with the Spirit and depending on God to save them would understand and be blessed by what he was saying. He was speaking to Christians under siege in that day, persecuted, thrown to the lions, burned as human torches to light Nero's garden party. If, as some claim today, (Evangelical dispensationalists) John was writing this to future generations, the whole letter makes no sense at all. How would it comfort you to hear about what God was going to do millenniums in the future, when you were being tortured right now?

John in fact, said; "Blessed is he who reads aloud the words of the prophecy, and blessed are those who hear, and who keep what is written therein; for the time is near." Revelation 1:3, RSV. Jonathan Mitchell translates the verse this way: "Happy (Blessed; Prosperous) is the one constantly reading (retrieving knowledge from), and those constantly hearing, the words of the prophecy and habitually keeping watch over (guarding; observing) the things having been written within it, for the situation is close at hand (or: for the season or occasion is near)." You will find the books he has translated on his website.

The bottom line here is that the book of Revelation is

revealing the Christ to us, in us and through us. It is something for the here and now, not afar off. If I tell you, "Jake, the time for me to come to your house for dinner is near at hand," you would not assume you had thousands of years or even a month to get your food purchased and prepared. You'd get right on it. Likewise, John's readers understood that the ancient symbols he used to convey his message of hope, grace, and triumph in God, was for them right then, in the fires of tribulation where they found themselves.

Similarly, in Matthew 24, *when Jesus was talking about the cataclysmic events that were coming: wars and rumors of wars, tribulation, betrayal, false prophets, the abomination in the Holy place spoken of by* Daniel: 6-15, *and gross wickedness so evil and traumatic that unless God shortened the days for the elect's sake, no flesh would be saved vs. 22, He said it would shortly come upon them. Note Verse 34: "Truly, I say to you, this generation will not pass away till all these things take place." RSV. That would indicate that all these horrific things would come to pass within forty years, (the designated number of years in a generation) or else there are some extremely old Jews hiding out on the planet someplace. In fact, within a generation of the time Jesus spoke this, His words were fulfilled on the 9th of Av, (July on our calendar) when the Roman general Titus sacked Jerusalem, destroyed the magnificent temple Herod the Great had built, and burned all the records.*

When the soldiers put the image of Caesar (whom they considered a god in the flesh), on a spear and stood it in the Holy Place, the abomination of desolation had taken place on earth. That was AD 70. It's over, finished, done with! There's no need for a third temple to be built to carry this prophecy out, as dispensationalists insist... Herod's temple was the one in which it already happened. John's readers knew precisely what he was talking about. Jesus' disciples knew exactly what He was talking about as well.

Titus was so incensed at the fight the Jews put up, and about how long it took to bring them down, that he ordered all the Christians to be killed along with the Jews. But Jesus' words saved them, for He had warned them, "When you see the armies circling the city, run for your lives. Don't go back home for anything. If you are in the fields, flee, and if you are on the roof tops get out of there!" Luke 21:20-24. (Jan's version). They did as He said, and not a Christian could be found in the city of Jerusalem when it finally toppled. Also as Jesus had prophesied, there was not one stone left on another Luke 21:6. In fact, the only thing left of the beautiful temple Herod the Great built, finished just a few years prior to AD 70, is the Western Wall, formerly called the Wailing Wall, where devout Jews pray today.

I know you have struggled with this for a long time, Jake, and my prayer is that God will remove the veil from your eyes that you might see the truth, hidden by the doctrines of men, and dogmas of religion and translation errors. All of that is good for Church coffers, profitable to the organization in terms of money and service, but horrific on the souls of men and women longing to be set free from fear.

We love you and stand with you in your search for truth. I really like the Recovery New Testament translation of this verse: "But when He, the Spirit of reality, comes, He will guide you into all the reality; for He will not speak from Himself, but what He hears He will speak; and He will declare to you the things that are coming." John 16:13. The only reality in the entire Universe and beyond is Christ Himself. We can't look to our life, our politics, our education, or our Church to show us reality, for only He is real. On the other side of the Lake of Fire is our Father, "For from Him and through Him and to Him are all things." Romans 11:36.

Father, reveal Yourself to all who still fear the fire and dread the coming punishment threatened by some who don't really know You as You are. We thank You and bless You that the Holy Spirit and fire are Your gifts to us, transforming us into Your image and likeness, causing us to be reflectors of Your glory to the waiting world. Amen. Love you, Jan and Lenny.

36

Reflectors Of Your Glory

I am almost certain that by now, your theological world has been rocked or at least challenged as mine has! Through this process, hopefully and prayerfully you have been encouraged to take a few new steps of faith. Stepping away from a religious system of controlling influence enabled me to embrace a new found freedom that I could not have had otherwise.

True freedom brings a new perspective and responsibility that allows for us to respectfully come under the Lordship of Jesus Christ in a whole new kind of way. As we acquire the mind of Christ while under His Lordship, our lives will change in such a way, that over time we will be able to reflect more of the Glory given to Him by His Father. The depth of our relationship to God our Father through His Son Jesus Christ, will be directly related to the amount of glory each of us will be privileged to carry in the eternal ages to come. I believe that ruling and reigning, ranking and positioning, and the giving and taking of rewards is somehow related to the amount of glory God will allow for us to carry and reflect as He predetermines, by the degree of our relationship with Him.

By coming to know God our Father through His Son Jesus Christ, we can begin making excellent choices as to how we ought to live our lives in every circumstance. I cannot emphasize enough, the extreme importance of understanding these principles while it is yet day!

If you are feeling your heart being pulled into Gods grace, that's His mercy being extended toward you. He loves you and is calling you back to Himself. All that is required of you to do–is respond to His love. God is perfectly capable of saving you. *Believe on the Lord Jesus Christ, and you will be saved.* Acts 16: 31. *I have not come to call the righteous, but sinners to repentance.* Luke 5:32. *If you then, being evil, know how to give good gifts to your children, how much more will your Heavenly Father give the Holy Spirit to those who ask Him.* Luke 11:13. *If you confess with your mouth the Lord Jesus Christ and believe in your heart that God raised Him from the dead you will be saved.* Romans 10:9.

We have come to the end of an amazing journey together, yet in reality it is just the beginning of an awesome opportunity to explore the vast riches of a wonderful heritage that awaits each of us. I have written passionately with all sincerity concerning the truths of God's incomprehensible, and totally amazing redeeming love.

When it is all said and done, evil will have served its ultimate purpose in creation. It will be known by all, that evil was the surgical instrument of precision in the hand of a sovereign, loving, and merciful God.

Through the atoning work of Jesus Christ our Redeemer, we are being perfected to a degree, depth, and quality that could not have come about otherwise. It was God our loving Father's plan from before the very beginning of time to lower us into the realm of carnality, so that we all could be resurrected into a new realm of spiritual perfection. Thank God for His never failing love. Amen!

37

Something To Think About

That which has been before, will be again. There is nothing new under the sun. God has put eternity in our hearts, so set your mind on things above, for your life is hidden with Christ. We are His workmanship created for good works that God prepared beforehand. He has not revealed to us yet what we shall be, but His thoughts are of peace and for our future. We can receive nothing unless it is given to us from Heaven. Our Father hides revelation from the wise, and gives to the babes, as His Son wills. Many prophets and Kings desire to see and understand what you see, and what you hear, but they cannot. Solid food belongs to us, so let us exercise our senses. Let's leave the elementary principles, and move on to perfection. Abba Father designed eternal quality into our substance, so let us honor one another by preferring the needs and interests of others over our own. Tests are absolutely necessary in our lives, because of God's eternal plans and purposes for us, His children. It is time to depart from the basic elementals of our salvation. Our Father is infinitely more interested in the new man that Christ is forming in us. Redemption gives us the ability to overcome. May you be blessed in hearing what the Spirit is saying. (See Ecclesiastes 1:9, 10; Ecclesiastes 3:11 - 14; Ecclesiastes 6:10; Colossians 3:1-5; Ephesians 2:10; 1 John 3:2; Jeremiah 29:11; John 3:27; Luke 10:21-24; Hebrews 5:14; Hebrews 6:1-3).

O give thanks to the Lord, for He is good! For His mercy endures forever. Psalm 107:1.

The Lord is good to all, and His tender mercies are over all His works. Psalm 145:9.

For I will not contend for ever, nor will I always be angry; for the spirit would fail before Me, and the souls which I have made. Isaiah 57:16.

For God did not send His Son into the world to condemn the world, but to save the world through Him. John 3:17.

The last enemy that will be destroyed is death. 1 Corinthians 15:26.

This is a faithful saying and worthy of all acceptance. For to this end we both labor and suffer reproach, because we trust in the living God, who is the Savior of all men especially of those who believe. These things command and teach. 1 Timothy 4:9-11.

And every creature which is in Heaven and on the earth and under the earth and such as are in the sea, and all that are in them, I heard saying: Blessing and honor and glory and power be to Him who sits on the throne and to the Lamb, forever and ever! Revelation 5:13.

And I heard a loud voice in Heaven saying, "Behold, the tabernacle is with men, and He will dwell with them, and they shall be His people. God Himself will be with them and be their God. And God will wipe away every tear from their eyes; there shall be no more death, nor sorrow, nor crying. There shall be no more pain, for the former things have passed away." Then He who sat on the throne said, "Behold, I make all things new." And He said to me, "Write, for these words are true and faithful." Revelation 21:3-5.

Closing Remarks

Throughout the ages of time gathering information was extremely difficult, due to the fact that most information was passed along by oral tradition or by laborious individual hand written copies. Only the educated could read, so the masses had no choice but to depend on the privileged to instruct, preach, or teach, until the invention of the printing press.

The dissemination of information improved greatly after the advent of the printing press, but the bulk of information was still tightly controlled by the ruling class, and by those in religious authority.

With the advent of the computer and instant "everything," we no longer have an excuse not to be able to research something thoroughly out ourselves. There are many excellent resources available at our fingertips enabling us to become experts in any field of choice. Even a child can access complex information and make sense of it in today's world.

We are encouraged in Scripture to "test all things" and to "hold onto that which is good." I also encourage you to test the things that have been shared from the pages of this book. I have only scratched the surface of what is in my heart to share. There are countless others that have written similar books concerning God's unfailing love–going much deeper than I ever could myself. Go ahead, do some research, take your time and taste and see that the Lord is good! May God bless you all.

All net proceeds from the sale of this book will be reinvested into the ongoing work of proclaiming the good news of Jesus Christ to as many people as possible. Countless numbers of individuals desperately need to hear that their sins are not being held against them. God's love is unfailing, and will accomplish all of His eternal purposes, to His glory. Amen!

Rev. Hank Van Zyderveld

End Notes

1) Heaven: Alcorn, Randy C. Available through Tyndale House Publishers, Inc. Copyright © 2004 by Eternal Perspective Ministries. All rights reserved. (Chapter 2.)
2) In The Garden. C. Austin Miles, 1912. (Chapter 3.)
3) Some of what I wrote about regarding being in "The School Of Suffering," were gleaned, paraphrased, and re-blended into a common thought from the writings of Paul E. Billheimer from his book titled; "Don't Waste Your Sorrows," published by Kingsway Publications Ltd, Lottbridge Drove, Eastbourne, E. Sussex BN23 6NT by Richard Clay (The Chaucer Press) Ltd, Bungay, Suffolk. Typeset by Nuprint Services Ltd. Harpenden, Herts. (Chapter 19.)
4) The writings of T. Austin Sparks are available for free re-distribution from the public domain. (Chapter 21.)
5) "God's Plan For All" is a book written by David and Zoe Sulem, a Christian married couple living in England. The book is available as a free download from their web site. http://www.godsplanforall.com/ (Chapter 23.)
6) The writings of A.P. Adams are available for free re-distribution from the public domain. (Chapter 30.)
7) "Send In The Flame" by Lenny Antonsson is available from "The Glory Road, a Kingdom Highway" Jan & Lenny Antonsson 17178 Highway 59, Neosho, MO. 64850 USA http://thegloryrd.com/ used with permission. (Chapter 32.)

8) "The Primrose Path To Gehenna" by Jan Austin Antonsson is available from "The Glory Road, a Kingdom Highway" Jan & Lenny Antonsson 17178 Highway 59, Neosho, MO. 64850 USA http://thegloryrd.com/ used with permission. (Chapter 33.)

9) Notes: A. The Emphatic Diaglott is an interlinear word For word translation of the Greek Text into English. (Chapter 33.)

   B. http://www.tentmaker.org. Or for those without Internet access, Gary and Michelle can be reached at Tentmaker, 118 Walnut, Hermann, MO 65401. Upon request, they will send you free of charge, a list of their articles and publications, including the Origin and History of the doctrine of Endless Punishment.

   C. I think this is a marvellous exposition of passages which struck terror into my heart as a young person. I knew that there was another explanation of them, but until I saw this discussion, I was unsure what it was.

   D. In this passage, the word which is translated Hell is Hades, which in the literal Greek means unseen.

   E. This word translated Hell is Tartarus. See reference above from "Origin and History of the Doctrine of Endless Punishment."

   F. The word Hades appears here in the Greek. According to the appendix, Hades means that which is in darkness, hidden, invisible, or obscure.

   G. The man in Jesus' parable was cast out of the presence of the king into bitter darkness as a result of insisting on wearing his own garments instead of those provided for him.

   H. From "The Best From A.P. Adams," published by Treasures of Truth, PO Box 99, Eagle ID. 83636.

10) "Hell Is A Four Letter Word" by Jan Austin Antonsson is available from "The Glory Road, a Kingdom Highway" Jan & Lenny Antonsson 17178 Highway 59, Neosho, MO. 64850 USA http://thegloryrd.com/ used with permission. (Chapter 34.)

11) "The Other Side Of The Lake Of Fire" by Jan Antonsson is available from "The Glory Road, a Kingdom Highway" Jan & Lenny Antonsson 17178 Highway 59, Neosho, MO. 64850 USA http://thegl ryrd.com/ used with permission. (Chapter 35.)

Resources

Amirault Gary, Is Salvation A Deliverance From Hell or Eternal Death? http://www.what-the-hell-is-hell.com/FromHellsEternalDeath.htm

Antonsson Jan & Lenny, The Glory Road, a Kingdom Highway. 17178 Highway 59, Neosho, MO. 64850 USA http://the-gloryrd.com/

Baer Jackson, What The Hell. How did we get it so wrong? Eternity, grace, and the message of love. All Rights Reserved. Copyright © 2011 Outskirts Press, Inc. http://www.outskirtspress.com

Beauchemin Gerry with D. Scott Reichard, Hope Beyond Hell The Righteous Purpose Of God's Judgment. © 2007. 2010 All Rights Reserved. Malista Press Olmito.

Bell Rob, Love Wins. Harper Collins e-books

Everly Bob, At The End Of The Ages... The Abolition of Hell. © 2002,2003 All rights reserved.

Ferwerda Julie, Raising Hell Christianity's Most Controversial Doctrine Put Under Fire. All rights reserved. Vagabond Group (PO Box 1001, Lander, WY 82520.

Herring T.A., Scandalous Grace, How Christianity Came To Believe In A God Whose Love Is Impotent, A Savior Who Fails To Save The World, And A Hell That Wins Most Souls. Copyright 2010 T.A. Herring.

MacDonald Gregory, The Evangelical Universalist. Copyright © 2006 Wipf & Stock, 199 W. 8th Ave. Eugene, Or 97401.

Purcell Purcell Ph. D., Spiritual Terrorism Spiritual Abuse from the Womb to the Tomb Author House.™ 1663 Liberty Drive, Suite 200 Bloomington, IN 47403 www.author-house.com

Roach Elwin & Margit, The Pathfinder. PO Box 4004 Alamogordo, NM 88311-4004 http://www.godfire.net/

Sulem David & Zoe, God's Plan For All. Please visit there site and read their book Available as a free down load! http://www.godsplanforall.com/

Talbott Thomas, The Inescapable Love Of God. Universal Publishers/uPublish.com © 1999, revised printing 9/2002 USA

Talbott Thomas, Universal Salvation? The Current Debate. © 2004 in the United States of America by Wm. B. Eerdmans Publishing Co. 255 Jeffereson Ave. S.E., Grand Rapids, Michigan 49503/P.O.Box 163, Cambridge CB3 9PU U.K. www.eerdmans.com